2nd Workshop on Natural Language Processing for Social Media

(SocialNLP 2014)

Held at COLING 2014

Dublin, Ireland
24 August 2014

ISBN: 978-1-63439-227-3

Printed from e-media with permission by:

Curran Associates, Inc.
57 Morehouse Lane
Red Hook, NY 12571

CURRAN ASSOCIATES INC.
proceedings
.com

Some format issues inherent in the e-media version may also appear in this print version.

Printed by Curran Associates, Inc. (2014)

For permission requests, please contact the Association for Computational Linguistics at the address below.

Association for Computational Linguistics
209 N. Eighth Street
Stroudsburg, Pennsylvania 18360

Phone: 1-570-476-8006
Fax: 1-570-476-0860

acl@aclweb.org

Additional copies of this publication are available from:

Curran Associates, Inc.
57 Morehouse Lane
Red Hook, NY 12571 USA
Phone: 845-758-0400
Fax: 845-758-2634
Email: curran@proceedings.com
Web: www.proceedings.com

Introduction

Welcome to the COLING 2014 Second Workshop on Natural Language Processing for Social Media (SocialNLP). SocialNLP is a new inter-disciplinary area of natural language processing (NLP) and social computing. We consider three plausible directions of SocialNLP: (1) addressing issues in social computing using NLP techniques; (2) solving NLP problems using information from social networks or social media; and (3) handling new problems related to both social computing and natural language processing.

Through this workshop, we anticipate to provide a platform for research outcome presentation and head-to-head discussion in the area of SocialNLP, with the hope to combine the insight and experience of prominent researchers from both NLP and social computing domains to contribute to the area of SocialNLP jointly. Also, selected and expanded versions of papers presented at SocialNLP will be published in two follow-on Special Issues of Springer Cognitive Computation (CogComp) and the International Journal of Computational Linguistics and Chinese Language Processing (IJCLCLP).

The submissions to this year's workshop were again of high quality and we had a competitive selection process. We received 18 submissions, and due to a rigorous review process, we only accepted 6 of them. Thus the acceptance rate was 33%. We also have 2 invited papers. The workshop papers cover a broad range of SocialNLP-related topics, such as aspect extraction, multi-lingual sentiment analysis, sentiment feature selection, online rating prediction, sentiment sequence recognition, automatic identification, verbal behavior and persuasiveness analysis, and user classification. We had a total of 18 reviewers. We warmly thank our PC members for the timely reviews and constructive comments.

We are delighted to have Prof. Paolo Rosso, from Universitat Politecnica de Valencia, as our keynote speaker.

We especially thank the Workshop Committee Chairs Dr. Jennifer Foster, Prof. Dan Gildea, and Prof. Tim Baldwin, and Local Co-Chair Dr. John Judge.

We hope you enjoy the workshop!

SocialNLP organizers
Shou-de Lin, Lun-Wei Ku, Erik Cambria, and Tsung-Ting Kuo
August 24, 2014
Dublin, Ireland

Organizers:

Shou-de Lin, National Taiwan University
Lun-Wei Ku, Academia Sinica
Erik Cambria, Nanyang Technological University
Tsung-Ting Kuo, National Taiwan University

Program Committee:

Berlin Chen, National Taiwan Normal University
Hsin-Hsi Chen, National Taiwan University
Amitava Das, Samsung Research India
Dipankar Das, National Institute of Technology
Min-Yuh Day, Tamkang University
Jennifer Foster, Dublin City University
June-Jei Kuo, National Chung Hsing University
Chuan-Jie Lin, National Taiwan Ocean University
Rafal Rzepka, Hokkaido University
Yohei Seki, University of Tsukuba
Ker-Yih Su, Behavior Design Corp
Ming-Feng Tsai, National Cheng Chi University
Hsin-Min Wang, Academia Sinica
Jenq-Haur Wang, National Taipei University of Technology
Yejun Wu, Louisiana State University
Yungfang Wu, Peking University
Yunqing Xia, Tsinghua University
Ruifeng Xu, Harbin Institute of Technology Shenzhen Graduate School

Invited Speaker:

Paolo Rosso, Universitat Politecnica de Valencia (Spain)

Invited Papers:

Carlos Argueta and Yi-Shin Chen, "Multi-Lingual Sentiment Analysis of Social Data Based on Emotion-Bearing Patterns"
Soujanya Poria, Erik Cambria, Lun-Wei Ku, Chen Gui and Alexander Gelbukh, "A Rule-Based Approach to Aspect Extraction from Product Reviews"

Table of Contents

Workshop Program

2014/08/24

09:30 Opening

Keynote Speech

09:35 *SocialIrony*
Paolo Rosso

10:30 Coffee Break

Regular Presentation 1

11:00 *Feature Selection for Highly Skewed Sentiment Analysis Tasks*
Can Liu, Sandra Kübler and Ning Yu

11:30 *"My Curiosity was Satisfied, but not in a Good Way": Predicting User Ratings for Online Recipes*
Can Liu, Chun Guo, Daniel Dakota, Sridhar Rajagopalan, Wen Li, Sandra Kübler and Ning Yu

12:00 *Automatic Identification of Arabic Language Varieties and Dialects in Social Media*
Fatiha Sadat, Farzindar Kazemi and Atefeh Farzindar

12:30 Lunch

Invited Presentation

14:00 *A Rule-Based Approach to Aspect Extraction from Product Reviews*
Soujanya Poria, Erik Cambria, Lun-Wei Ku, Chen Gui and Alexander Gelbukh

14:30 *Multi-Lingual Sentiment Analysis of Social Data Based on Emotion-Bearing Patterns*
Carlos Argueta and Yi-Shin Chen

15:00 Coffee Break

2014/08/24 (continued)

Regular Presentation 2

15:30	*Recognition of Sentiment Sequences in Online Discussions* Victoria Bobicev, Marina Sokolova and Michael Oakes
16:00	*Verbal Behaviors and Persuasiveness in Online Multimedia Content* M. Chatterjee, S. Park, H.S. Shim, K. Sagae and L.-P. Morency
16:30	*Content+Context for Twitter User Classification* William Campbell, Elisabeth Baseman and Kara Greenfield
17:00	Closing

SocialIrony

Paolo Rosso
PRHLT Research Center
Universitat Politecnica de Valencia (Spain)
Associate Professor
prosso@dsic.upv.es

Abstract

In ironic texts what is literally said is usually negated, and in absence of an explicit negation marker. This makes social computing quite challenging. Detecting irony is very much important for NLP tasks such as polarity classification, sentiment analysis, opinion mining, or reputation analysis. There is a growing interest from the research community in investigating the impact of irony on polarity classification and sentiment analysis. A tasks will be organised at SemEval in 2015 on Sentiment Analysis of Figurative Language in Twitter (http://alt.qcri.org/semeval2015/task11). What are the linguistic patterns that users employ in social media in order to try to be ironic in just maybe 140 characters? Linguistic devices that go beyond positive or negative polarity such as ambiguity, incongruity, unexpectedness and emotional contexts have an important role as triggers of irony. In the talk I will describe how irony is employed in social media texts (Twitter, Amazon, Facebook etc.) and what are the recent state-of-the-art attempts for its automatic detection. At the end of the talk, I will address also the even more challenging and fine-grained problem of distinguishing among irony, sarcasm and satire: e.g. If you find it hard to laugh at yourself, I would be happy to do it for you.

Proceedings of the Second Workshop on Natural Language Processing for Social Media (SocialNLP), page 1,
Dublin, Ireland, August 24 2014.

Feature Selection for Highly Skewed Sentiment Analysis Tasks

Can Liu
Indiana University
Bloomington, IN, USA
liucan@indiana.edu

Sandra Kübler
Indiana University
Bloomington, IN, USA
skuebler@indiana.edu

Ning Yu
University of Kentucky
Lexington, KY, USA
ning.yu@uky.edu

Abstract

Sentiment analysis generally uses large feature sets based on a bag-of-words approach, which results in a situation where individual features are not very informative. In addition, many data sets tend to be heavily skewed. We approach this combination of challenges by investigating feature selection in order to reduce the large number of features to those that are discriminative. We examine the performance of five feature selection methods on two sentiment analysis data sets from different domains, each with different ratios of class imbalance.

Our finding shows that feature selection is capable of improving the classification accuracy only in balanced or slightly skewed situations. However, it is difficult to mitigate high skewing ratios. We also conclude that there does not exist a single method that performs best across data sets and skewing ratios. However we found that $TF * IDF_2$ can help in identifying the minority class even in highly imbalanced cases.

1 Introduction

In recent years, sentiment analysis has become an important area of research (Pang and Lee, 2008; Bollen et al., 2011; Liu, 2012). Sentiment analysis is concerned with extracting opinions or emotions from text, especially user generated web content. Specific tasks include monitoring mood and emotion; differentiating opinions from facts; detecting positive or negative opinion polarity; determining opinion strength; and identifying other opinion properties. At this point, two major approaches exists: lexicon and machine learning based. The lexicon-based approach uses high quality, often manually generated features. The machine learning-based approach uses automatically generated feature sets, which are from various sources of evidence (e.g., part-of-speech, n-grams, emoticons) in order to capture the nuances of sentiment. This means that a large set of features is extracted, out of which only a small subset may be good indicators for the sentiment.

One major problem associated with sentiment analysis of web content is that for many topics, these data sets tend to be highly imbalanced. There is a general trend that users are willing to submit positive reviews, but they are much more hesitant to submit reviews in the medium to low ranges. For example, for the YouTube data set that we will use, we collected comments for YouTube videos from the comedy category, along with their ratings. In this data set, more than 3/4 of all ratings consist of the highest rating of 5. For other types of user generated content, they opposite may be true.

Heavy skewing in data sets is challenging for standard classification algorithms. Therefore, the data sets generally used for research on sentiment analysis are balanced. Researchers either generate balanced data sets during data collection, by sampling a certain number of positive and negative reviews, or by selecting a balanced subset for certain experiments. Examples for a balanced data set are the movie review data set (Pang and Lee, 2004) or the IMDB review data set (Maas et al., 2011). Using a balanced data set allows researchers to focus on finding robust methods and feature sets for the problem. Particularly, the movie review data set has been used as a benchmark data set that allows for comparisons of various sentiment analysis models. For example, Agarwal and Mittal (2012), Agarwal and Mittal (2013), Kummer

Proceedings of the Second Workshop on Natural Language Processing for Social Media (SocialNLP), pages 2–11,
Dublin, Ireland, August 24 2014.

and Savoy (2012), O'Keefe and Koprinska (2009), and Paltoglou and Thelwall (2010) all proposed competitive feature selection methods evaluated on the movie review data set. However, the generalizability of such feature selection methods to imbalanced data sets, which better represent real world situations, has not been investigated in much detail. Forman (2003) provides an extensive study of feature selection methods for highly imbalanced data sets, but he uses document classification as task.

This current paper investigates the robustness of three feature selection methods that Forman (2003) has shown to be successful, as well as two variants of $TF * IDF$. The three methods are Odds-Ratio (OR), Information Gain (IG), and Binormal Separation (BNS). BNS has been found to perform significantly better than other methods in more highly skewed tasks (Forman, 2003). The two variants of $TF * IDF$ differ in the data set used for calculating document frequency. We investigate the behavior of these methods on a subtask of sentiment analysis, namely the prediction of user ratings. For this, we will use data sets from two different domains in order to gain insight into whether or not these feature selection methods are robust across domains and across skewing ratios: One set consists of user reviews from Epicurious[1], an online community where recipes can be exchanged and reviewed, the other set consists of user reviews of YouTube comedy videos.

The remainder of this paper is organized as follows: In section 2, we explain the rationale for applying feature selection and introduce the feature selection methods that are examined in this paper. Section 3 introduces the experimental settings, including a description of the two data sets, data preprocessing, feature representation, and definition of the binary classification tasks. In section 4, we present and discuss the results for the feature selection methods, and in section 5, we conclude.

2 Feature Selection and Class Skewing

In a larger picture, feature selection is a method (applicable both in regression and classification problems) to identify a subset of features to achieve various goals: 1) to reduce computational cost, 2) to avoid overfitting, 3) to avoid model failure, and 4) to handle skewed data sets for classification tasks. We concentrate on the last motivation, even though an improvement of efficiency and the reduction of overfitting are welcome side effects. The feature selection methods studied in this paper have been used in text classification as well, which is a more general but similar task using n-gram features. However, since all measures are intended for binary classification problems, we reformulate the rating prediction into a binary classification problem (see section 3.5).

Feature selection methods can be divided into wrapper and filter methods. Wrapper methods use the classification outcome on a held-out data set to score feature subsets. Standard wrapper methods include forward selection, backward selection, and genetic algorithms. Filter methods, in contrast, use an independent measure rather than the error rate on the held-out data. This means that they can be applied to larger feature sets, which may be unfeasible with wrapper methods. Since sentiment analysis often deals with high dimensional feature representation, we will concentrate on filter methods for our feature selection experiments.

Previous research (e.g. (Brank et al., 2002b; Forman, 2003)) has shown that Information Gain and Odds Ratio have been used successfully across different tasks and that Binormal Separation has good recall for the minority class under skewed class distributions. So we will investigate them in this paper. Other filter methods are not investigated in this paper due to two main concerns: We exclude Chi-squared and Z-score, statistical tests because they require a certain sample size. Our concern is that their estimation for rare words may not be accurate. We also exclude Categorical Proportion Difference and Probability Proportion Difference since they do not normalize over the sample of size of positive and negative classes. Thus, our concern is that they may not provide a fair estimate for features from a skewed data sets.

2.1 Notation

Following Zheng et al. (2004), feature selection methods can be divided into two groups: one-sided and two-sided measures. One-sided measures assign a high score to positively-correlated features and a low

[1] www.epicurious.com

score to negative features while two-sided measures prefer highly distinguishing features, independent of whether they are positively or negatively correlated. Zheng et al. (2004) note that the ratio of positive and negative features affects precision and recall of the classification, especially for the minority class. For one-sided methods, we have control over this ratio by selecting a specified number of features one each side; for two-sided methods, however, we do not have this control. In this paper, we will keep a 1:1 ratio for one-sided methods. For example, if we select 1 000 features, we select the 500 highest ranked features for the positive class, and the 500 highest ranked features for the negative class. When using two-sided methods, the 1 000 highest ranked features are selected.

For the discussion of the feature selection methods, we use the following notations:

- S: target or positive class.
- $\overline{S}$: negative class.
- D_S: The number of documents in class S.
- $D_{\overline{S}}$: The number of documents in class $\overline{S}$.
- D_{Sf}: The number of documents in class S where feature f occurs.
- $D_{\overline{S}f}$: The number of documents in class $\overline{S}$ where feature f occurs.
- T_{Sf}: The number of times feature f occurs in class S.

2.2 Feature Selection Methods

In addition to Information Gain, Odds Ratio and Bi-Normal Separation, $TF * IDF$ is included for comparison purposes. We define these measures for binary classification as shown below.

Information Gain (IG): IG is a two-sided measure that estimates how much is known about an unobserved random variable given an observed variable. It is defined as the entropy of one random variable minus the conditional entropy of the observed variable. Thus, IG is the reduced uncertainty of class S given a feature f:

$$IG = H(S) - H(S|f) = \sum_{f\in\{0,1\}} \sum_{S\in\{0,1\}} P(f,S) log \frac{P(f,S)}{P(f)P(S)}$$

Brank et al. (2002b) analyzed feature vector sparsity and concluded that IG prefers common features over extremely rare ones. IG can be regarded as the weighted average of Mutual Information, and rare features are penalized in the weighting. Thus they are unlikely to be chosen (Li et al., 2009). Forman (2003) observed that IG performs better when only few features (100-500) are used. Both authors agreed that IG has a high precision with respect to the minority class.

Odds Ratio (OR): OR (Mosteller, 1968) is a one-sided measure that is defined as the ratio of the odds of feature f occurring in class S to the odds of it occurring in class $\overline{S}$. A value larger than 1 indicates that a feature is positively correlated with class S, a value smaller than 1 indicates it is negatively correlated:

$$OR = log \frac{P(f,S)(1 - P(f,S))}{P(f,\overline{S})(1 - P(f,\overline{S}))}$$

Brank et al. (2002b) showed that OR requires a high number of features to achieve a given feature vector sparsity because it prefers rare terms. Features that occur in very few documents of class S and do not occur in $\overline{S}$ have a small denominator, and thus a rather large OR value.

Bi-Normal Separation (BNS): BNS (Forman, 2003) is a two-sided measure that regards the probability of feature f occurring in class S as the area under the normal distribution bell curve. The whole area under the bell curve corresponds to 1, and the area for a particular feature has a corresponding threshold along the x-axis (ranging from negative infinite to positive infinite). For a feature f, one can find the threshold that corresponds to the probability of occurring in the positive class, and the threshold corresponding to the probability of occurring in $\overline{S}$. BNS measures the separation in these two thresholds:

$$BNS = |F^{-1}(\frac{D_{Sf}}{D_S}) - F^{-1}(\frac{D_{\overline{S}f}}{D_{\overline{S}}})|$$

where F^{-1} is the inverse function of the standard normal cumulative probability distribution. As we can see, the F^{-1} function exaggerates an input more dramatically when the input is close to 0 or 1 which means that BNS perfers rare words.

Term Frequency * Inverse Document Frequency (TF*IDF): $TF * IDF$ was originally proposed for information retrieval tasks, where it measures how representative a term is for the document in which it occurs. When $TF * IDF$ is adopted for binary classification, we calculate the $TF * IDF$ of a feature w.r.t. the positive class (normalized) and the $TF * IDF$ w.r.t. the negative class (normalized). We obtain the absolute value of the difference of these two measures. If a feature is equally important in both classes and thus would not contribute to classification, it receives a small value. The larger the value, the more discriminative the feature. We apply two variants of $TF * IDF$, depending on how IDF is calculated:

$$TF * IDF_1 = (0.5 + \frac{0.5 \times T_{Sf}}{max_i(T_{Sf_i})}) \times log(\frac{D_S + D_{\overline{S}}}{D_{Sf}})$$

$$TF * IDF_2 = (0.5 + \frac{0.5 \times T_{Sf}}{max_i(T_{Sf_i})}) \times log(\frac{D_S}{D_{Sf}})$$

In the first variant, $TF * IDF_1$, document frequency is based on the whole set of examples while in the second variant, $TF * IDF_2$, document frequency is based only on the class under consideration, S.

3 Experimental Setup

3.1 Data Sets

Epicurious Data Set: We developed a web crawler to scrape user reviews for 10 146 recipes, published on the Epicurious website before and on April 02, 2013. On the website, each recipe is assigned a rating of 1 to 4 forks, including the intermediate values of 1.5, 2.5, and 3.5. This is an accumulated rating over all user reviews. (Reviews with ratings of 0 were excluded, they usually indicate that recipes have not received any ratings.) We rounded down all the half ratings, e.g., 1.5 forks counts as 1 fork, based on the observation that users are generous when rating recipes. Our experiments classify each recipe by aggregating over all its reviews. While a little more than half of the recipes received 1 to 10 reviews, there are recipes with more than 100 reviews. To avoid an advantage for highly reviewed recipes, we randomly selected 10 reviews if a recipe has more than 10 reviews. Recipes with less than 3 reviews were eliminated since they do not provide enough information. After these clean-up steps, the data set has the distribution of ratings shown in table 1.

YouTube Data Set: Using the Google YouTube Data API, we collected average user ratings and user comments for a set of YouTube videos in the category *Comedy*. Each video is rated from 1 to 5. The distribution of ratings among all YouTube videos is very skewed, as illustrated in figure 1. Most videos are rated highly; very few are rated poorly. The 1% quantile is 1.0; the 6.5% quantile is 3.0; the 40% quantile is 4.75; the 50% quantile is 4.85; and the 77% quantile is 5.0. We selected a set of 3 000 videos. Videos with less than 5 comments or with non-English comments are discarded.

rating	no.
1 fork	44 recipes
2 forks	304 recipes
3 forks	1416 recipes
4 forks	1368 recipes

Table 1: The distribution of ratings in the Epicurious data set.

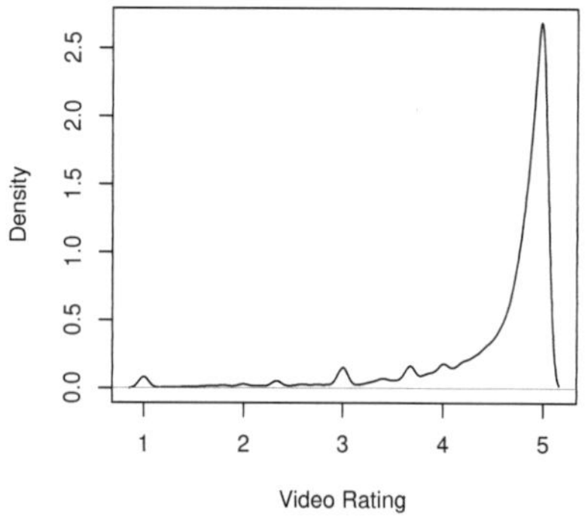

Figure 1: Skewing in the YouTube data set.

3.2 Data Preprocessing

Before feature extraction, basic preprocessing is conducted for both data sets individually. For the Epicurious data set, we perform stemming using the Porter Stemmer (Porter, 1980) to normalize words, and rare words ($\leq$ 4 occurrences) are removed. On the YouTube data set, we perform spelling correction and normalization because the writing style is rather informal. Our normalizer collapses repetitions into their original forms plus a suffix "RPT", thus retaining this potentially helpful clue for reviewer's strong emotion without increasing the features due to creative spelling. For example, "loooooove" is changed to "loveRPT" and"lolololol" to "lolRPT". The normalizer also replaces all emoticons by either"EMOP" for positive emoticons or "EMON" for negative emoticons. Besides a standard English dictionary, we also use the Urban Dictionary[2] since it has a better coverage of online abbreviations.

We do not filter stop words for two reasons: 1) Stop words are domain dependent, and some English stop words may be informative for sentiment analysis, and 2) uninformative words that are equally common in both classes will be excluded by feature selection if the method is successful.

3.3 Feature representation

Since our focus is on settings with high numbers of features, we use a bag-of-words approach, in which every word represents one feature, and its term frequency serves as its value. Different feature weighting methods, including binary weighting, term frequency, and $TF{*}IDF$ have been adopted in past sentiment analysis studies (e.g., (Pang et al., 2002; Paltoglou and Thelwall, 2010)). (Pang et al., 2002) found that simply using binary feature weighting performed better than using more complicated weightings in a task of classifying positive and negative movie reviews. However, movie reviews are relatively short, so there may not be a large difference between binary features and others. Topic classification usually uses term frequency as feature weighting. $TF * IDF$ and variants were shown to perform better than binary weighting and term frequency for sentiment analysis (Paltoglou and Thelwall, 2010).

Since our user rating prediction tasks aggregate all user comments into large documents and predict ratings per recipe/YouTube video, term frequency tends to capture richer information than binary fea-

[2]http://www.urbandictionary.com/

Epicurious			YouTube		
ratio	no. NEG	no. POS	ratio	no. NEG	no. POS
1:8	348	2 784	1:10	56	559
1:1.57	348	547	1:1.57	356	559
1:1	348	348	1:1	559	559

Table 2: Skewing ratios and sizes of positive and negative classes for both data sets.

tures. Thus, we use term frequency weighting for simplicity, not to deviate from the focus of feature selection methods. Since there is a considerable variance in term frequency in the features, we normalize the feature values to [0,1] to avoid large feature values from dominating the vector operations in classifier optimization.

For the Epicurious data, the whole feature set consists of 10 677 unigram features. For YouTube, the full feature set of features consists of 23 232 unigram features. We evaluate the performance of feature selection methods starting at 500 features, at a step-size of 500. For the Epicurious data, we include up to 10 500 features. For the YouTube data, we stop at 15 000 features due to prohibitively long classification times.

3.4 Classifier

The classifier we use in this paper is Support Vector Machines (SVMs) in the implementation of SVM^{light} (Joachims, 1999). Because algorithm optimization is not the focus of this study, we use the default linear kernel and other default parameter values. Classification results are evaluated by accuracy as well as precision and recall for individual classes.

3.5 Binary Classification

Since all feature selection methods we use in our experiments are defined under a binary classification scenario, we need to redefine the rating prediction task. For both data sets, this means, we group the recipes and videos into a *positive* and a *negative* class. A baseline classifier predicts every instance as the majority class. For both data sets, the majority class is *positive*.

For the Epicurious data set, 1-fork and 2-fork recipes are grouped into the negative class (NEG), and 3-fork and 4-fork recipes are grouped into the positive class (POS), yielding a data set of 348 NEG and 2 784 POS recipes (skewing ratio: 1:8). The different skewing ratios we use are shown in table 2. $2/3$ of the data is used for training, and $1/3$ for testing, with the split maintaining the class ratio. Note that for the less skewed settings, all NEG instances were kept while POS instances were sampled randomly.

For the YouTube data set, we sample from all videos with rating 5 for the positive class and from all videos with ratings between and including 1 and 3 for the negative class. This yields 559 POS and 559 NEG videos. The different skewing ratios we use are shown in table 2. $7/8$ of the data is used for training, and $1/8$ for testing, with the split maintaining the class ratio.

4 Results

4.1 Results for the Epicurious Data Set

The results for the Epicurious data set with different skewing ratios are shown in figure 2. The accuracy of the baseline is 50% for the 1:1 ratio, 61% for 1:1.57, and 88.9% for 1:8.

The results show that once we use a high number of features, all the feature selection methods perform the same. This point where they conflate is reached at around 4 000 features for the ratios of 1:1 and 1:1.57. There, accuracy reaches around 71%. For the experiment with the highest skewing, this point is reached much later, at around 8 000 features. For this setting, we also reach a higher accuracy of around 89%, which is to be expected since we have a stronger majority class. Note that once the conflation point is reached, the accuracy also corresponds to the accuracy when using the full feature set. This accuracy is always higher than that of the baseline.

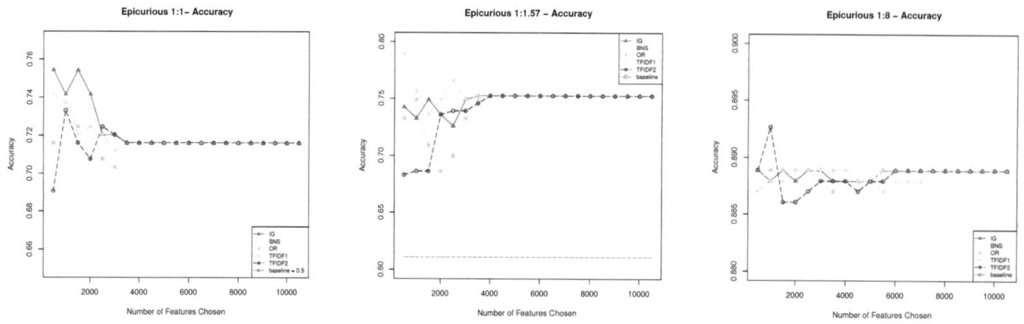

Figure 2: The results for the Epicurious data set.

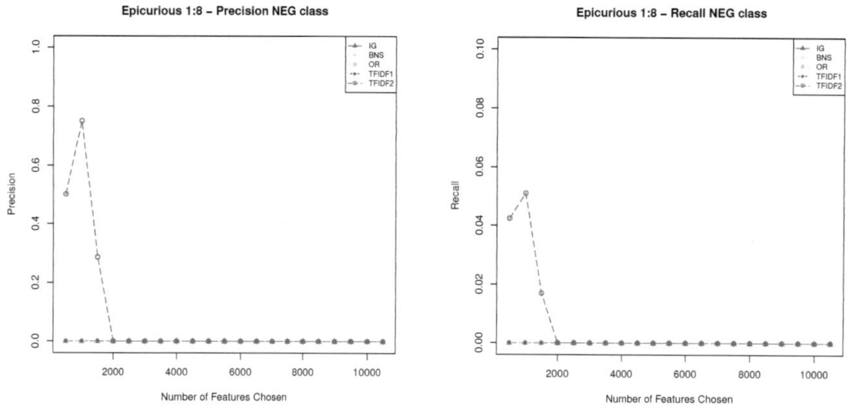

Figure 3: Precision and recall for the negative cases in the Epicurious set, given a 1:8 skewing.

The results also show that the most pronounced differences between feature selection methods occur in the balanced data set. In the set with the highest skewing, the differences are minor, and only $TF * IDF_2$ improves over the baseline when using 1 000 features.

Another surprising result is that $TF * IDF_2$, OR, and BNS have a tendency to fluctuate between higher and lower results than the setting using all features. This means that it is difficult to find a good cut-off point for these methods. $TF * IDF_1$ and IG show clear performance gains for the balanced setting, but they also show more fluctuation in settings with higher skewing.

From these results, we can conclude that for sentiment analysis tasks, feature selection is useful only in a balanced or slightly skewed cases if we are interested in accuracy. However, a look at the precision and recall given the highest skewing (see figure 3) shows that $TF * IDF_2$ in combination with a small number of features is the only method that finds at least a few cases of the minority class. Thus if a good performance on the minority class examples is more important than overall accuracy, $TF * IDF_2$ is a good choice. One explanation is that $TF * IDF_2$ concentrates on one class and can thus ignore the otherwise overwhelming positive class completely. $TF * IDF_1$ and OR have the lowest precision, and BNS fluctuates. Where recall is concerned, $TF * IDF_1$ and IG reach the highest recall given a small feature set.

4.2 Results for the YouTube Data Set

The results for the YouTube data set with different skewing ratios are shown in figure 4. The accuracy of the baseline is 50% for the 1:1 ratio, 61.08% for 1:1.57, and 90.9% for 1:10.

The results show that even though the YouTube data set is considerably smaller than the Epicurious one, is does profit from larger numbers of selected features: For the balanced and the low skewing, there

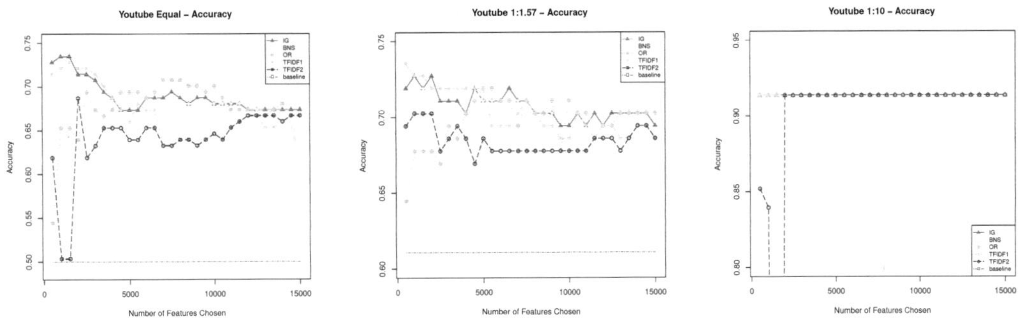

Figure 4: The results for the YouTube set.

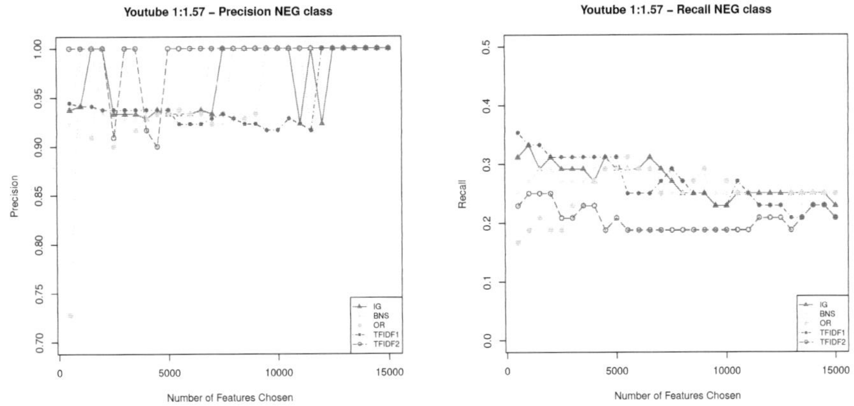

Figure 5: Precision and recall for the negative cases in the YouTube set, given a 1:1.57 skewing.

is no point at which the methods conflate. The results for the highly skewed case show that no feature selection method is capable of finding cases of the minority class: all methods consistently identify only one instance of the negative class. However, this may be a consequence of the small data set. In terms of accuracy, we see that a combination of a small number of features with either IG or $TF * IDF_1$ provides the best results. For the YouTube data set, BNS also performs well but requires a larger set of features for reaching its highest accuracy. We assume that this is the case because BNS has a tendency to prefer rare words. Note that we did not test for number of features greater than 15 000 because of the computation cost, but we can see that the performance curve for different feature selection methods tends to conflate to the point that represents the full feature set.

If we look at the performance of different feature selection methods on identification of minority class instances, we find that $TF * IDF_2$ again manages to increase recall in the highly skewed case, but this time at the expense of precision. For the 1:1.57 ratio, all methods reach a perfect precision when a high number of features is selected, see figure 5. $TF * IDF_2$ is the only method that reaches this precision with small numbers of features, too. However, this is not completely consistent.

4.3 Discussion

If we compare the performance curves across data sets and skewing ratios and aim for high accuracy, we see that there is no single feature selection method that is optimal in all situations. Thus, we have to conclude that the choice of feature selection method is dependent on the task. In fact, the performance of a feature selection method could depend on many factors, such as the difficulty of the classification task, the preprocessing step, the feature generation decision, the data representation scheme (Brank et al., 2002a), or the classification model (e.g., SVM, Maximum Entropy, Naive Bayes).

We have also shown on two different data sets, each with three skewing ratios, that it is difficult for feature selection methods to mitigate the effect of highly skewed class distributions while we can still improve performance by using a reduced feature set for slightly skewed cases. Thus, the higher the skewing of the data set is, the more difficult it is to find a feature selection method that has a positive effect, and parameters, such as feature set size, have to be optimized very carefully. Thus, feature selection is much less effective in highly skewed user rating tasks than in document classification.

However, if the task requires recall of the minority class, our experiments have shown that $TF * IDF_2$ is able to increase this measure with a small feature set, even for highly imbalanced cases.

5 Conclusion and Future Work

In this paper, we investigated whether feature selection methods reported to be successful for document classification perform robustly in sentiment classification problems with a highly skewed class distribution. Our findings show that feature selection methods are most effective when the data sets are balanced or moderately skewed, while for highly imbalanced cases, we only saw an improvement in recall for the minority class.

In the future, we will extend feature selection methods – originally defined for binary classification scenarios – to handle multi-class classification problems. A simple way of implementing this is be to break multi-class classification into several 1-vs.-all or 1-vs.-1 tasks, perform feature selection on these binary tasks and then aggregate them. Another direction that we want to take is integrating more complex features, such as parsing or semantic features, into the classification task to investigate how they influence feature selection. In addition, we will compare other approaches against feature selection for handling highly skewed data sets, including classification by rank, ensemble learning methods, and memory-based learning with a instance-specific weighting. Finally, a more challenging task is to select features for sentiment analysis problems where no annotation (feature selection under unsupervised learning) or few annotations (feature selection under semi-supervised learning) are available.

References

Basant Agarwal and Namita Mittal. 2012. Categorical probability proportion difference (CPPD): A feature selection method for sentiment classification. In *Proceedings of the 2nd Workshop on Sentiment Analysis where AI meets Psychology (SAAIP)*, pages 17–26.

Basant Agarwal and Namita Mittal. 2013. Sentiment classification using rough set based hybrid feature selection. In *Proceedings of the 4th Workshop on Computational Approaches to Subjectivity, Sentiment & Social Media Analysis (WASSA)*, pages 115–119, Atlanta, GA.

Johan Bollen, Huina Mao, and Xiao-Jun Zeng. 2011. Twitter mood predicts the stock market. *Journal of Computational Science*, 2:1–8.

Janez Brank, Marko Grobelnik, Nataša Milic-Frayling, and Dunja Mladenic. 2002a. An extensive empirical study of feature selection metrics for text classification. In *Proceedings of the Third International Conference on Data Mining Methods and Databases for Engineering, Finance and Other Fields*, Bologna, Italy.

Janez Brank, Marko Grobelnik, Nataša Milic-Frayling, and Dunja Mladenic. 2002b. Feature selection using Linear Support Vector Machines. Technical Report MSR-TR-2002-63, Microsoft Research.

George Forman. 2003. An extensive empirical study of feature selection metrics for text classification. *Journal of Machine Learning Research*, 3:1289–1305.

Thorsten Joachims. 1999. Making large-scale SVM learning practical. In B. Schölkopf, C. Burges, and A. Smola, editors, *Advances in Kernel Methods - Support Vector Learning*. MIT-Press.

Olena Kummer and Jaques Savoy. 2012. Feature selection in sentiment analysis. In *Proceeding of the Conférence en Recherche d'Infomations et Applications (CORIA)*, pages 273–284, Bordeaux, France.

Shoushan Li, Rui Xia, Chengqing Zong, and Chu-Ren Huang. 2009. A framework of feature selection methods for text categorization. In *Proceedings of the Joint Conference of the 47th Annual Meeting of the ACL and the 4th International Joint Conference on Natural Language Processing of the AFNLP*, pages 692–700, Suntec, Singapore.

Bing Liu. 2012. *Sentiment Analysis and Opinion Mining*. Synthesis Lectures on Human Language Technologies. Morgan & Claypool Publishers.

Andrew L. Maas, Raymond E. Daly, Peter T. Pham, Dan Huang, Andrew Y. Ng, and Christopher Potts. 2011. Learning word vectors for sentiment analysis. In *Proceedings of the 49th Annual Meeting of the Association for Computational Linguistics: Human Language Technologies*, pages 142–150, Portland, OR.

Frederick Mosteller. 1968. Association and estimation in contingency tables. *Journal of the American Statistical Association*, 63(321):1–28.

Tim O'Keefe and Irena Koprinska. 2009. Feature selection and weighting methods in sentiment analysis. In *Proceedings of the 14th Australasian Document Computing Symposium (ADCS)*, pages 67–74, Sydney, Australia.

Georgios Paltoglou and Mike Thelwall. 2010. A study of information retrieval weighting schemes for sentiment analysis. In *Proceedings of the 48th Annual Meeting of the Association for Computational Linguistics*, pages 1386–1395, Uppsala, Sweden.

Bo Pang and Lillian Lee. 2004. A sentimental education: Sentiment analysis using subjectivity summarization based on minimum cuts. In *Proceedings of the 42nd Annual Meeting on Association for Computational Linguistics*, Barcelona, Spain.

Bo Pang and Lillian Lee. 2008. Opinion mining and sentiment analysis. *Foundations and Trends in Information Retrieval*, 2(1-2):1–135.

Bo Pang, Lillian Lee, and Shivakumar Vaithyanathan. 2002. Thumbs up? Sentiment classification using machine learning techniques. In *Proceedings of the 2002 Conference on Empirical Methods in Natural Language Processing (EMNLP)*, pages 79–86, Philadelphia, PA.

Martin Porter. 1980. An algorithm for suffix stripping. *Program*, 14(3):130—137.

Zhaohui Zheng, Xiayun Wu, and Rohini Srihari. 2004. Feature selection for text categorization on imbalanced data. *ACM SIGKDD Explorations Newsletter*, 6(1):80–89.

"My Curiosity was Satisfied, but not in a Good Way": Predicting User Ratings for Online Recipes

Can Liu, Chun Guo, Daniel Dakota , Sridhar Rajagopalan, Wen Li, Sandra Kübler
Indiana University
{liucan, chunguo, ddakota, srrajago, wl9, skuebler}@indiana.edu

Ning Yu
University of Kentucky
ning.yu@uky.edu

Abstract

In this paper, we develop an approach to automatically predict user ratings for recipes at Epicurious.com, based on the recipes' reviews. We investigate two distributional methods for feature selection, Information Gain and Bi-Normal Separation; we also compare distributionally selected features to linguistically motivated features and two types of frameworks: a one-layer system where we aggregate all reviews and predict the rating vs. a two-layer system where ratings of individual reviews are predicted and then aggregated. We obtain our best results by using the two-layer architecture, in combination with 5 000 features selected by Information Gain. This setup reaches an overall accuracy of 65.60%, given an upper bound of 82.57%.

1 Introduction

Exchanging recipes over the internet has become popular over the last decade. There are numerous sites that allow us to upload our own recipes, to search for and to download others, as well as to rate and review recipes. Such sites aggregate invaluable information. This raises the question how such sites can select good recipes to present to users. Thus, we need to automatically predict their ratings.

Previous work (Yu et al., 2013) has shown that the reviews are the best rating predictors, in comparison to ingredients, preparation steps, and metadata. In this paper, we follow their approach and investigate how to use the information contained in the reviews to its fullest potential. Given that the rating classes are discrete and that the distances between adjacent classes are not necessarily equivalent, we frame this task as a classification problem, in which the class distribution is highly skewed, posing the question of how to improve precision and recall especially for the minority classes to achieve higher overall accuracy. One approach is to identify n-gram features of the highest discriminating power among ratings, from a large number of features, many of which are equally distributed over ratings. An alternative strategy is to select less surface-oriented, but rather linguistically motivated features. Our second question concerns the rating predictor architecture. One possibility is to aggregate all reviews for a recipe, utilizing rich textual information at one step (one-layer architecture). The other possibility is to rate individual reviews first, using shorter but more precise language clues, and then aggregate them (two-layer). The latter approach avoids the problem of contradictory reviews for a given review, but it raises the question on how to aggregate over individual ratings. We will investigate all these approaches.

The remainder of the paper is structured as follows: First, we review related work in section 2. Then, in section 3, we motivate our research questions in more detail. Section 4 describes the experimental setup, including the data preparation, feature extraction, classifier, and evaluation. In section 5, we present the results for the one-layer experiments, and in section 6 for the two-layer experiments. Section 7 investigates a more realistic gold standard. We then conclude in section 8.

2 Related Work

This section provides a brief survey for sentiment analysis on online reviews.

Proceedings of the Second Workshop on Natural Language Processing for Social Media (SocialNLP), pages 12–21, Dublin, Ireland, August 24 2014.

During the last decade or more, there has been significant body of sentiment analysis studies on online reviews. Two major approaches exist: lexicon-based and machine learning. A lexicon-based approach requires prior knowledge of important sentiment features to build a list of sentiment-bearing words (or phrases), which are often domain independent. Examples of such lexicons include the Multi-Perspective Question Answering (MPQA) subjectivity lexicon (Wilson et al., 2005) and the Linguistic Inquiry and Word Count (LIWC) dictionary (Pennebaker et al., 2014). The sentiment of a review is determined by various ways of aggregating information about the sentiment-bearing words (phrases), such as their frequency and sentiment scores. The machine learning approach dominantly adopts supervised learning algorithms, which treat sentiment analysis as a text classification task. In this case, sentiment features are generated from a pre-labeled corpus. Given the lack of annotated data, semi-supervised learning is adopted (Yu, 2014; Yu and Kübler, 2011). For this study, we focus on a specific language domain of online recipe reviews, which has user ratings, thus we choose supervised learning. We also adopt one existing linguistic lexicon to provide extra features for our classification models.

The earliest sentiment analysis on online reviews was done by Pang et al. (2002); they applied several supervised learning algorithms to classify online movie reviews into a positive and a negative class. This study found that machine learning methods outperformed human annotators. It also found that bigrams did not improve the classification performance, whether used alone or with unigrams, which has been confirmed by many following studies. However, Cui et al. (2006) later conjectured that when the training corpus is large enough, adding bigrams to unigrams improved the accuracy of binary product review classification. A great number of diverse features were proven to be beneficial to capture subtle sentiments across studies and a "kitchen sink" approach is often adopted for sentiment analysis (Yang et al., 2008). However, when features are noisy and redundant, researcher have found it beneficial to identify the most telling ones (Gamon, 2004; Ng et al., 2006).

While it is useful to differentiate positive and negative reviews, a finer level of distinction can help users better compare online reviews. As a matter of fact, even extra half star ratings can have dramatic economic impact (Anderson and Magruder, 2012). To predict multi-level ratings, either multiclass classification or regression methods can be applied (Koppel and Schler, 2006; Yu et al., 2013). Pang and Lee (2005) have also proposed an alternative meta-algorithm based on metric labeling for predicting three or four sentiment classes for movie reviews. In their experiments, the meta-algorithm outperformed SVMs in either one-versus-all or regression mode. In order to adopt this meta-algorithm, however, one needs to determine an effective review similarity measure, which is not always straightforward.

If an item receives multiple reviews and/or comes from multiple sources, an overall rating needs to be generated for this item. Yu et al. (2013) generated this overall rating by treating all the reviews from one recipe as one long review. In this study, we are going to investigate how to integrate review-level rating predictions to generate a recipe-level prediction. Rating aggregation has been studied intensively for collaborative filtering, where the user/rater's bias is adjusted (e.g., the trustworthy user's rating has more influence than others (McGlohon et al., 2010)). Since our current study does not take raters' information into consideration, we are going to stay with the sample aggregation method. A study by Garcin et al. (2009) suggests that among mean, median, and mode, the median is often a better choice as it is not as sensitive to outliers as the mean.

3 Research Questions

As described in the previous section, many studies use only word unigrams or bigrams. We use word and part-of-speech (POS) n-grams, with n ranging from 1 to 3. This approach generates a large number of features, creating a very noisy and high dimensional data set, which also makes classifier training and testing slow. For this reason, we first investigate the effect of feature selection. The next question concerns the usefulness of linguistically and socio-linguistically motivated features. This results in a small, but ideally meaningful set of features. The last research question that we approach in this paper concerns whether classifying recipes on the recipe level is too coarse. In general, we have a wide range of reviews, each of which is accompanied by a user rating. Thus, it is possible to conduct review-level classification and then aggregate the ratings.

3.1 Feature Selection

Our primary feature set is based on word and POS n-grams. This results in an extremely large feature set of 449 144 features, many of which do not serve any discriminatory function. A common first step to trimming the feature set is to delete stop words. However, in the cooking domain, it is unclear whether stop words would help. Feature selection is used to identify n-grams tightly associated with individual ratings. Additionally, a extremely high dimensional feature representation makes model training and testing more time consuming, and is likely to suffer from overfitting - given a large number of parameters needed to describe the model. Due to the exponential computation time required by wrapper approaches for feature selection, we use filtering approaches which are based on statistics about the distribution of features. Previous research (Liu et al., 2014) indicates that Bi-Normal Separation (BNS) (Forman, 2003) and Information Gain (IG) yield best results for this task. Information Gain is defined as follows:

$$IG = H(S) - H(S|f) = \sum_{f\in\{0,1\}} \sum_{S\in\{0,1\}} P(f,S)log\frac{P(f,S)}{P(f)P(S)}$$

where S is the positive class, f a feature, and $P(f,S)$ the joint probability of the feature f occurring with class S. Bi-Normal Separation finds the separation of the probability of a feature occurring in the positive class vs. the negative class, normalized by F^{-1}, which is the inverse function of the standard normal cumulative probability distribution. Bi-Normal Separation is defined as follows:

$$BNS = |F^{-1}(\frac{D_{Sf}}{D_S}) - F^{-1}(\frac{D_{\overline{S}f}}{D_{\overline{S}}})|$$

where D_S is the number of documents in class S, $D_{\overline{S}}$ the number of documents in class $\overline{S}$, D_{Sf} the number of documents in class S where feature f occurs, and $D_{\overline{S},f}$ the number of documents in class $\overline{S}$ where feature f occurs. The F^{-1} function exaggerates an input more dramatically when the input is close to 0 or 1, which means that BNS prefers rare words.

Since both metrics are defined for binary classification, the features are chosen in terms of a separation of the recipes into "bad" ratings (1-fork and 2-fork) versus "good" ratings (3-fork and 4-fork), on the assumption that the selected features will be predictive for the more specific classes as well. For review-based experiments, the features are chosen with regard to "good" and "bad" individual reviews.

3.2 Linguistically Motivated Features

Linguistic features In order to examine whether linguistic information can improve prediction accuracy, linguistically motivated features were extracted from the data. We selected seven features based on the assumption that they reveal a sense of involvedness or distance of the reviewer, i.e., that authors distance themselves from a recipe to indicate negative sentiment and show more involvedness to indicate positive sentiment. These seven features are:

1. The percentage of personal pronouns per sentence.
2. The number of words per sentence.
3. The total number of words in the review.
4. The percentage of passive sentences per review.
5. The number of punctuation marks per sentence.
6. The number of capitalized characters per sentence.
7. The type/token ratio per review.

Features such as words per sentence, total words, and the type/token ratio are seen as indicating the complexity of the review.

Our hypothesis is that the longer the review, the more likely it indicates a negative sentiment as the review may go at lengths to indicate why something was negative.

Similarly, using the passive voice can be viewed as distancing oneself from the review indicating a sense of impartial judgement, most likely associated with negativity, as one tends to actively like something (i.e. "We liked it" versus "It wasn't well seasoned."). Since some reviews with strong emotions are written in all capital letters as well as contain many punctuation marks (particularly "!"), these features are also collected as possible indicators of sentiment.

Lexicon-based features In addition, we used an existing lexicon, the Linguistic Inquiry and Word Count (LIWC) dictionary (Pennebaker et al., 2014), to analyze several emotional and cognitive dimensions in the recipe reviews. This lexicon is chosen over other sentiment lexicons because it covers a broad range of categories beyond simply positive and negative emotions. Briefly, it contains general descriptor categories (e.g., percentage of words captured by the dictionary), standard linguistic dimensions (e.g., percentage of words in the text that are pronouns), word categories tapping psychological constructs (e.g., biological processes), personal concern categories (e.g., work), spoken language dimensions (e.g., accent), and punctuation categories. Details of these dimensions can be found in the LIWC 2007 manual.

For our study, we first extracted all the features from a review set independent from our training/test set. We then selected the LIWC features with highest power to differentiate four rating classes based on Information Gain. Below are the 15 selected features. Note that the linguistic features here are document-level features, not sentence-level features, as proposed above.

- Linguistic Processes
  - *Negations* (e.g., never, no): 57 words
  - *1st person plural* (e.g., we, us): 12 words
  - *Exclamation mark*
- Psychological Processes
  - *Affective process*: this high level category contains 915 positive/negative emotions, anxiety, anger and sadness related terms.
  - *Positive emotion* (e.g., love, nice, sweet): 406 words
  - *Negative emotion* (e.g., hurt, ugly, nasty): 499 words
  - *Sadness* (e.g., crying, grief): 101 words
  - *Exclusive* (e.g., but, exclude): 17 words
  - *Tentative* (e.g., maybe, perhaps, guess): 155 words
  - *Causation* (e.g., because, hence): 108 words
  - *Discrepancy* (e.g., should, would, could) : 76 words
  - *Certainty* (e.g., always, never): 83 words
  - *Sexual* (e.g., love): 96 words
  - *Feel* (e.g., feel, touch): 75 words
- Personal Concerns
  - *Leisure* (e.g, cook, chat, movie): 229 words

It is not surprising that emotion related features are selected, but it is interesting to see that cognitive processes features (i.e., *causation*, *tentative*, *discrepancy*, *certainty* and *exclusive*) are also highly related to ratings. Taking a close look at the means of feature values across four ratings, we observe that people tend to use words in the *tentative*, *discrepancy*, *exclusive* categories when they write negative recipe reviews. For terms in *causation*, however, it is the opposite: People write about reasons when writing positive reviews. Some further investigation is needed to explain why this is the case. We also see that the higher the rating, the more likely it is that people use first person plural pronouns. This may be due to the fact that only when people like a recipe, they will tend to share the food with others. Other observations

1 fork	108
2 fork	787
3 fork	5 648
4 fork	3 546

Table 1: The distribution of ratings in the Epicurious data.

include: The *sexual* features are positively correlated with high ratings, which is mainly due to the word "love" in its non-sexual meaning. People tend to use more words from the perception processes category *feel* when they complain about a recipe.

3.3 One-Layer Prediction Versus Two-Layer Prediction

The one-layer or recipe-based approach consider all reviews per recipe as a single document. This approach has rich textual information, especially when a large number of reviews exist for a recipe. However, the concern with this approach is that the reviews in themselves may be varied. There are recipes whose reviews range from the lowest to the highest rating. Given such a range of individual ratings, we can assume that the recipe-based approach will be faced with a contradictory feature set for certain recipes. For this reason, we also investigate a two-layer or review-based approach. Here, every individual review is rated automatically. In a second step, we aggregate over all reviews per recipe. Aggregation can either take the form of majority voting, average, or of a second classifier which takes the aggregated ratings as features to make a final decision. However, this approach will suffer from often very short reviews, which do not allow the extraction of sufficient features as well as from the inequality in the number of reviews per recipe.

4 Experimental Setup

4.1 Data Set

We scraped user reviews for 10 089 recipes, published on the Epicurious website[1] before and on April 02, 2013. Typically, a recipe contains three parts: ingredients, cooking instructions, and user reviews. In our experiments, we focus exclusively on the reviews. Each user review has a rating for this recipe, ranging from 1 fork to 4 forks. There is also an overall rating per recipe, which is the average of all reviews ratings as well as ratings submitted without reviews. Half forks are possible for recipe rating but not for review ratings. These recipes were pre-processed to remove reviews with zero ratings. Recipes that had no reviews were then subsequently removed. In order to counter the effect of the wide variance in the number of reviews per recipe, we randomly sampled 10 reviews from recipes with more than 10 reviews. We had performed initial experiments with all reviews, which resulted in only minor differences. At the review level, rare words (unigrams occurring less than four times) were removed for two reasons: 1) Extremely rare words are likely to be noise rather than sentiment-bearing clues; 2) the feature selection method BNS is biased towards rare words; 3) such words do not generalize well. The recipes were then tagged using the Stanford POS Tagger (Toutanova et al., 2003).

The data set is severely skewed with regard to the number of recipes per fork: Users seem to be more willing to review good recipes. To lessen the effect of imbalance in the rating classifier, all half fork reviews were added to their corresponding full star reviews (i.e., 1.5 fork was added to the 1 fork data). This resulted in the data split of 10 089 recipes shown in table 1. Even after collapsing the half stars, there is still a very large skewing of the data towards the higher ratings. This means, feature selection is important to mitigate the imbalance to a certain degree.

4.2 Features

In addition to the linguistic features described in section 3.2, we also extracted n-gram features: word unigrams, bigrams, and trigrams as well as POS tag unigrams, bigrams, and trigrams. Since the data

[1] http://www.epicurious.com

Method	750	900	1 000	1 500	3 000	6 000
BNS	–	–	31.33	–	42.00	50.67
IG	62.00	62.00	**62.33**	**62.33**	61.00	58.67

Table 2: Results for feature selection based on Bi-Normal Separation (BNS) and Information Gain (IG).

includes tokens particular to the web, modifications were made to the data to help with the processing of these types of tokens. URLs were replaced with a single URL token and tagged with a unique "URL" tag. Emoticons were defined as either positive or negative and subsequently replaced by EMOP or EMON respectively. Since it is unclear for this task whether more frequent feature should receive a larger weight, we normalized features values to a range of [0,1].

4.3 Classifiers

Preliminary experiments were run to determine the best classifier for the task. We decided on Support Vector Machines in the implementation of SVM multi-class V1.01 (Crammer and Singer, 2002) for both review-level and recipe-level rating prediction. Initial experiments showed that SVM multi-class V1.01 reaches higher results on our skewed data set than the current V2.20. For this reason, all experiments reported in this paper are based on V1.01 with its default settings, i.e., using a linear kernel.

To aggregate review-level ratings into a recipe-level prediction, we experimented with both the maximum entropy classifier in the implementation of the Stanford Classifier (Manning and Klein, 2003) and the SVM multi-class classifier. We included Maxent Classifier because given the small number of features it is no longer clear whether SVM is advantageous.

4.4 Baseline

The baseline was established following Yu et al. (2013) as selecting the label of majority class (3-fork) to tag all recipes, producing an accuracy of 56.00% for both one-layer and two-layer systems.

4.5 Evaluation

Evaluation was performed using 3-fold cross validation. Since the data is skewed, we report Precision (P), Recall (R), and F-Scores (F) for all classes across each experiment, along with standard accuracy.

5 Results for One-Layer Prediction

5.1 Feature Selection

We first investigated the effect of feature selection, varying the number of included features from 750 to 6 000. Results for the two methods and different feature thresholds are shown in table 2. Since previous work (Liu et al., 2014) showed that BNS has a tendency to select infrequent n-grams and would need a larger number of features than IG to achieve good performance, we tested the higher ranges of 1 000, 3 000, 6 000 features. None of these experiments yields an accuracy higher than the baseline of 56.00%. On the other hand, the performance of Information Gain peaks at 1 000 and 1 500 features, and we reach an absolute increase in accuracy of 6.33%. Given these experiments, for all following experiments, we use the combination of Information Gain and 1 000 n-gram features.

5.2 Linguistically Motivated Features

Here, we test the contribution of the linguistically motivated features introduced in section 3.2. To allow a comparison to previous experiments, we report the baseline and the results for using Information Gain.

For the two sets of linguistically motivated features, we used the following combination of features:

1. Lexicon-based features (Lex) combined with linguistic features (Ling) (22 features).
2. Lexicon-based features (Lex) combined with the 1 000 features selected by Information Gain (IG) (1015 features).

	1 fork			2 fork			3 fork			4 fork			
	P	R	F	P	R	F	P	R	F	P	R	F	Acc.
Base	0.00	0.00	0.00	0.00	0.00	0.00	56.00	100.00	72.00	0.00	0.00	0.00	56.00
IG	33.33	1.00	2.00	31.33	12.00	17.33	66.00	73.67	69.67	58.33	58.00	58.00	62.33
Lex+Ling	0.00	0.00	0.00	0.00	0.00	0.00	56.00	100.00	72.00	0.00	0.00	0.00	56.00
IG+Lex	39.00	2.00	3.67	31.67	10.00	15.00	65.33	75.33	69.67	59.67	55.67	57.33	62.67
IG+Ling	0.00	0.00	0.00	32.00	3.33	6.00	63.67	81.00	71.33	62.67	49.67	55.33	**63.33**
IG+Lex+Ling	0.00	0.00	0.00	32.00	3.33	6.00	63.67	81.00	71.33	62.67	49.67	55.33	**63.33**

Table 3: Results for manually selected features.

	1 fork			2 fork			3 fork			4 fork			
no. feat.	P	R	F	P	R	F	P	R	F	P	R	F	Acc.
1000	61.57	58.11	59.79	53.70	37.42	44.11	63.04	42.14	50.51	71.30	89.08	79.20	67.80
2000	61.65	58.27	59.91	52.96	39.40	45.18	63.37	43.19	51.37	71.86	88.70	79.40	68.11
3000	62.50	58.51	60.44	52.98	40.88	46.15	62.90	44.49	52.12	72.45	88.10	79.51	68.34
4000	62.45	58.45	60.38	52.38	41.05	46.03	62.99	45.54	52.86	72.83	87.70	79.58	**68.46**
5000	62.32	57.00	59.54	51.66	41.17	45.82	62.21	46.15	52.99	73.05	87.24	79.52	68.31

Table 4: Results on individual reviews for the two-layer experiments.

3. Linguistic features (Ling) combined with the 1 000 features selected by Information Gain (IG) (1007 features).
4. A combination of all three sets of features (IG+Lex+Ling) (1022 features).

The results for these experiments are reported in table 3. These results show that a combination of the two sets of linguistically motivated features does not increase accuracy over the baseline. In fact, the classification is identical to the baseline, i.e., all recipes are grouped into the majority class of 3-fork. We assume that the linguistically motivated features are too rare to be useful. If we add the lexicon-based features to the ones selected by Information Gain, we reach a minimal improvement over only the IG features: accuracy increases from 62.33% to 62.67%. This increase is mostly due to a better performance on the minority class of 1 fork. If we add the 7 linguistic features to the IG features, we reach the highest accuracy of 63.33%. However, this is due to a more pronounced preference for selecting the majority class. Adding the lexicon-based features to this feature set does not give any further improvements.

6 Results for Two-Layer Prediction

In this section, we investigate the two-layer or review-based prediction. For these experiments, we performed feature selection on the individual reviews using IG. Adding the linguistically motivated features considerably decreased performance. We assume that these features do not generalize well on the shorter reviews.

Note that the task approached here is a difficult task since the recipe rating on Epicurious is not the average over all the ratings associated to the individual reviews but also includes ratings by user who did not write a review. If we average over all the sampled gold standard review ratings per recipe, we reach an accuracy of 82.57%. This is the upper bound that we can reach in these experiments.

6.1 Classifying Individual Reviews

First, we look at the phase in which individual reviews are classified. The results of this set of experiments is shown in table 4. Note that there are three important trends here: 1) The accuracy of the SVM classifier is higher than for classifying recipes. The comparison needs to be taken with a grain of salt because these are two different tasks. However, this is an indication that it is possible to reach higher results based on aggregating over individual reviews. 2) For this task, we reach the highest results by using 4 000 features, i.e., a considerably higher number of features than the optimal set for the recipe-based experiments, where 1 000 features sufficed. We suspect that we need more features in this setting because the individual reviews are shorter so that individual features do not generalize as well as for complete recipes. 3) The classification of individual reviews is less skewed than for complete recipes. The F-scores

		1 fork			2 fork			3 fork			4 fork			
no. f.	sys.	P	R	F	P	R	F	P	R	F	P	R	F	Acc.
1000	avg	44.64	36.98	40.45	60.00	23.03	33.28	75.72	51.91	61.59	52.38	86.01	65.11	61.48
	maxent	43.87	33.33	37.88	58.30	19.73	29.48	73.90	58.77	65.47	55.03	81.40	65.67	63.41
	svm	62.21	62.21	62.21	56.18	16.03	24.94	72.24	58.14	64.43	53.92	80.82	68.68	62.21
2000	avg	44.61	38.83	41.52	61.45	24.29	34.82	76.12	53.96	63.15	53.45	85.53	65.79	62.58
	maxent	43.17	34.27	38.21	61.47	21.23	31.56	74.43	60.93	67.01	56.27	80.93	66.38	64.58
	svm	63.29	63.29	63.29	56.53	16.79	25.89	72.65	60.32	65.91	55.14	80.26	65.37	63.29
3000	avg	42.71	38.86	40.69	61.08	26.57	37.03	75.62	54.33	63.23	53.71	84.60	65.71	62.64
	maxent	42.40	35.20	38.47	61.90	23.40	33.96	74.00	61.90	67.41	56.83	79.73	66.36	64.84
	svm	63.53	63.53	63.53	54.09	17.41	26.34	72.14	61.45	66.37	55.80	79.02	65.41	63.53
4000	avg	38.64	34.22	36.30	61.09	24.89	35.37	75.23	55.91	64.15	54.34	83.81	65.93	63.07
	maxent	38.37	31.47	34.58	60.67	22.47	32.79	73.80	63.03	67.99	57.47	79.00	66.54	65.16
	svm	64.03	64.03	64.03	52.92	17.53	26.33	72.24	62.85	67.22	56.51	78.17	65.60	64.03
5000	avg	39.23	37.05	38.11	59.20	24.89	35.05	75.38	56.25	64.42	54.54	83.64	66.03	63.23
	maxent	38.03	33.40	35.56	58.37	22.00	31.96	73.97	64.17	68.72	58.13	78.57	66.82	**65.60**
	svm	64.68	64.68	64.68	50.19	17.40	25.84	72.52	64.18	68.10	57.45	77.95	66.15	64.68

Table 5: Results on aggregating reviews for the two-layer experiments.

for the non-majority classes are considerably higher than in the recipe-based setting. Thus, we expect to obtain more balanced results across classes in the aggregation as well.

6.2 Predicting Recipe Ratings by Aggregating Reviews

When aggregating review predictions to recipe rating, we use three methods: 1) Taking the average of the review ratings from the previous step; 2) using SVM; and 3) using a maximum entropy classifier (Maxent), the Stanford Classifier. When calculating the average over review rating predictions, the final average is rounded up. The results are reported in table 5. When using SVM and the maximum entropy classifier, we use four features, corresponding to the four ratings. The feature values are calculated as the percentage of reviews from the target recipe that were assigned to this fork rating by our review-level classifier.

Overall, the maximum entropy classifier yields the best performance, independent of the number of features used for the review-level classifier. The highest performance we reach by using 5 000 features and the maximum entropy classifier. Calculating the average results in the worst performance. Although Epicurious calculates the average user ratings based on review ratings and singular ratings, keep in mind that we use at most 10 reviews per recipe, hence only capture part of the image. This may explain why simply calculating the average does not work well. When looking at the F-scores for each fork in table 5, however, the maximum entropy classifier produces lower performance than average and SVM classifier for the 1 fork and 2 fork classes. For 1 fork, SVM has the highest F-scores for different numbers of features, followed by the averaging approach while for 2 fork, the average approach produced the highest F-scores. One possible explanation is that recipes with lower ratings have relatively small numbers of reviews and thus may be less impacted by our sampling.

7 Towards a More Realistic Gold Standard

When we aggregate over the individual review rating using the average, the results are only slightly better than the one-layer results. For example, the best performance using the average reaches an accuracy of 63.23%, as opposed to the one-layer accuracy of 62.33% in table 2 (note that these settings use only IG features). One reason for this low performance is that Epicurious averages all review ratings to generate a recipe rating, independent of whether there is review attached to the rating or not. Since our text-based classifiers make their decisions only based on the reviews, the question is how well we actually predict the average rating if only ratings attached to reviews were used in the calculation. In this way, we can evaluate how well our approach works if we assume that all the information is available to the classifier.

Consequently, we calculated a new gold standard, averaging gold ratings of individual reviews in the recipe sample. We investigate this effect based on the two-layer setting where reviews are aggregated via averaging. The results of this set of experiments are shown in table 6 for the two-layer approach and in table 7 for the one-liner approach. We report results using the gold label based on the ratings from

sys.	1 fork P	R	F	2 fork P	R	F	3 fork P	R	F	4 fork P	R	F	Acc.
EPI	39.23	37.05	38.11	59.20	24.89	35.05	75.38	56.25	64.42	54.54	83.64	66.03	63.23
EPI-AVG	56.41	51.16	53.66	62.73	62.73	62.73	76.89	65.66	70.83	67.10	85.39	75.15	71.10

Table 6: Evaluation on a more realistic gold standard for two-layer experiments.

	1 fork P	R	F	2 fork P	R	F	3 fork P	R	F	4 fork P	R	F	Acc.
Base	0.00	0.00	0.00	0.00	0.00	0.00	52.00	100.00	68.00	0.00	0.00	0.00	52.00
IG	8.33	1.00	1.67	29.67	11.00	16.00	64.33	70.00	67.00	64.00	66.00	64.67	63.33
Lex+Ling	0.00	0.00	0.00	0.00	0.00	0.00	51.33	99.33	67.67	41.33	1.00	2.00	51.00
IG+Lex	11.00	1.00	2.00	29.00	9.67	14.67	64.00	70.33	67.00	64.00	65.33	64.67	63.33
IG+Ling	16.67	1.00	2.00	31.00	6.33	10.67	63.00	72.67	67.67	65.00	63.33	64.00	63.33
IG+Lex+Ling	16.67	1.00	2.00	31.33	6.67	11.00	63.00	72.67	67.33	65.00	63.33	64.00	63.33

Table 7: Evaluation on a more realistic gold standard for one-layer experiments.

Epicurious (EPI) and based on the new gold standard (EPI-AVG). These results show that based on this more realistic gold standard, averaging over the individual reviews results in an accuracy of 71.10%, however with an upper bound of 100% instead of 82.57%. The results for the on-layer experiments are not as sensitive to this new gold standard. The baseline, which loses 4%, shows that now, the task is more difficult. All combinations involving IG selected features reach an accuracy of 63.33%, the same as for the Epicurious gold standard (see table 3).

8 Conclusion and Future Work

In this study, we have explored various strategies for predicting recipe ratings based on user reviews. This is a difficult task due to systemic reasons, user bias, as well as exogenous factors: 1) There are user ratings that do not come with reviews, which means that they constitute hidden information for our classifiers (so that we have an upper bound of 82.57% in overall accuracy). 2) Ratings are not entirely supported by text, i.e., some ratings seem to be independent from the review text, due to user behavior (e.g., people tend to give higher ratings in good weather than in bad weather (Bakhshi et al., 2014)).

Our experiments suggest that a two-layer approach, which predicts review-level ratings and aggregates them for the recipe-level rating, reaches a higher accuracy than the one-layer approach that aggregates all reviews and predicts on the recipe level directly, with a 3.6% absolute improvement in accuracy. If we evaluate the two-layer results on a more realistic gold standard, we achieve an even higher increase of 12.3%.

Our experiments also suggest that with feature selection, automatically generated n-gram features can produce reasonable results without manually generated linguistic cues and lexicons, although the latter does show a slight improvement, especially for minority classes.

A few directions can be taken for our future study: 1) Handling short reviews with better methods for dealing with sparse features. 2) The feature selection is conducted within a binary classification scenario (1- and 2-forks vs. 3- and 4-forks). It is worth exploring the effect of feature selection within four 1 vs. all scenarios (i.e., 1-fork against the rest, etc.). 3) We will explore aspect-level sentiment classification to provide a finer-grained summary of the recipes.

References

Michael Anderson and Jeremy Magruder. 2012. Learning from the crowd: Regression discontinuity estimates of the effects of an online review database. *The Economic Journal*, 122:957–989.

Saeideh Bakhshi, Partha Kanuparthy, and Eric Gilbert. 2014. Demographics, weather and online reviews: A study of restaurant recommendations. In *Proceedings of the WWW conference*, Seoul, Korea.

Koby Crammer and Yoram Singer. 2002. On the algorithmic implementation of multiclass kernel-based vector machines. *Journal of Machine Learning Research*, 2:265–292.

Hang Cui, Vibhu Mittal, and Mayur Datar. 2006. Comparative experiments on sentiment classification for online product reviews. In *Proceedings of the 21st National Conference on Artificial Intelligence*, AAAI'06, pages 1265–1270, Boston, Massachusetts.

George Forman. 2003. An extensive empirical study of feature selection metrics for text classification. *Journal of Machine Learning Research*, 3:1289–1305.

Michael Gamon. 2004. Sentiment classification on customer feedback data: Noisy data, large feature vectors, and the role of linguistic analysis. In *Proceedings of the 20th International Conference on Computational Linguistics (COLING)*, pages 841–847, Geneva, Switzerland.

Florent Garcin, Boi Faltings, Radu Jurca, and Nadine Joswig. 2009. Rating aggregation in collaborative filtering systems. In *Proceedings of the Third ACM Conference on Recommender Systems*, pages 349–352, New York, NY.

Moshe Koppel and Jonathan Schler. 2006. The importance of neutral examples in learning sentiment. *Computational Intelligence Journal*, 22:100–109. Special Issue on Sentiment Analysis.

Can Liu, Sandra Kübler, and Ning Yu. 2014. Feature selection for highly skewed sentiment analysis tasks. In *Proceedings of the Second Workshop on Natural Language Processing for Social Media (SocialNLP)*, Dublin, Ireland.

Christopher Manning and Dan Klein. 2003. Optimization, maxent models, and conditional estimation without magic. Tutorial at HLT-NAACL 2003 and ACL 2003.

Mary McGlohon, Natalie Glance, and Zach Reiter. 2010. Star quality: Aggregating reviews to rank products and merchants. In *Proceedings of Fourth International Conference on Weblogs and Social Media (ICWSM)*, pages 114–121, Washington, DC.

Vincent Ng, Sajib Dasgupta, and S. M. Niaz Arifin. 2006. Examining the role of linguistic knowledge sources in the automatic identification and classification of reviews. In *Proceedings of COLING/ACL*, pages 611–618, Sydney, Australia.

Bo Pang and Lillian Lee. 2005. Seeing stars: Exploiting class relationships for sentiment categorization with respect to rating scales. In *Proceedings of the 43rd Annual Meeting on Association for Computational Linguistics*, ACL, pages 115–124, Ann Arbor, MI.

Bo Pang, Lillian Lee, and Shivakumar Vaithyanathan. 2002. Thumbs up?: Sentiment classification using machine learning techniques. In *Proceedings of the Conference on Empirical Methods in Natural Language Processing*, EMNLP, pages 79–86, Philadelphia, PA.

James Pennebaker, Roger Booth, and Martha Francis, 2014. *Linguistic inqury and word count: LIWC 2007 operator's manual.* `http://homepage.psy.utexas.edu/HomePage/Faculty/Pennebaker/Reprints/LIWC2007_OperatorManual.pdf`.

Kristina Toutanova, Dan Klein, Christopher Manning, and Yoram Singer. 2003. Feature-rich part-of-speech tagging with a cyclic dependency network. In *Proceedings of HLT-NAACL 2003*, pages 252–259, Edmonton, Canada.

Theresa Wilson, Janyce Wiebe, and Paul Hoffmann. 2005. Recognizing contextual polarity in phrase-level sentiment analysis. In *Proceedings of the Conference on Empirical Methods in Natural Language Processing*, pages 347–354, Vancouver, Canada.

Kiduk Yang, Ning Yu, and Hui Zhang. 2008. WIDIT in TREC2007 blog track: Combining lexicon-based methods to detect opinionated blogs. In *Proceedings of the 16th Text Retrieval Conference*, Gaithersburg, MD.

Ning Yu and Sandra Kübler. 2011. Filling the gap: Semi-supervised learning for opinion detection across domains. In *Proceedings of the Fifteenth Conference on Computational Natural Language Learning*, CoNLL, pages 200–209, Portland, OR.

Ning Yu, Desislava Zhekova, Can Liu, and Sandra Kübler. 2013. Do good recipes need butter? Predicting user ratings of online recipes. In *Proceedings of the IJCAI Workshop on Cooking with Computers*, Beijing, China.

Ning Yu. 2014. Exploring co-training strategies for opinion detection. *Journal of the Association for Information Science and Technology*.

Automatic Identification of Arabic Language Varieties and Dialects in Social Media

Fatiha Sadat
University of Quebec in Montreal, 201 President Kennedy, Montreal, QC, Canada
sadat.fatiha@uqam.ca

Farnazeh Kazemi
NLP Technologies Inc.
52 Le Royer Street W., Montreal, QC, Canada
kazemi@nlptechnologies.ca

Atefeh Farzindar
NLP Technologies Inc.
52 Le Royer Street W., Montreal, QC, Canada
farzindar@nlptechnologies.ca

Abstract

Modern Standard Arabic (MSA) is the formal language in most Arabic countries. Arabic Dialects (AD) or daily language differs from MSA especially in social media communication. However, most Arabic social media texts have mixed forms and many variations especially between MSA and AD. This paper aims to bridge the gap between MSA and AD by providing a framework for AD classification using probabilistic models across social media datasets. We present a set of experiments using the character n-gram Markov language model and Naive Bayes classifiers with detailed examination of what models perform best under different conditions in social media context. Experimental results show that Naive Bayes classifier based on character bi-gram model can identify the 18 different Arabic dialects with a considerable overall accuracy of 98%.

1 Introduction

Arabic is a morphologically rich and complex language, which presents significant challenges for natural language processing and its applications. It is the official language in 22 countries spoken by more than 350 million people around the world[1]. Moreover, the Arabic language exists in a state of diglossia where the standard form of the language, Modern Standard Arabic (MSA) and the regional dialects (AD) live side-by-side and are closely related (Elfardy and Diab, 2013). Arabic has more than 22 dialects; some countries share the same dialect, while many dialects may exist alongside MSA within the same Arab country.

Modern Standard Arabic (MSA) is the written form of Arabic used mostly in education and scripted speech; it is also the formal communication language. Spoken Arabic is often referred to as colloquial Arabic, dialects, or vernaculars. Thus. Arabic dialects (AD) or colloquial languages are spoken varieties of Arabic and the daily language of several people. Arabic dialects and MSA share a considerable number of semantic, syntactic, morphological and lexical features; however, these features have many differences (Al-Sabbagh and Girju, 2013).

Recently, considerable interest was given to Arabic dialects and the written varieties of Arabic found on social networking sites such as chats, micro-blog, blog and forums, which is the target research of sentiment analysis, opinion mining, machine translation, etc.

Social media poses three major computational challenges, dubbed by Gartner the 3Vs of big data: *volume, velocity, and variety*[2]. NLP methods, in particular, face further difficulties arising from the short, noisy, and strongly contextualised nature of social media. In order to address the 3Vs of social media, new language technologies have emerged, such as the identification and definition of users' language varieties and the translation to a different language, than the source.

---

[1] http://en.wikipedia.org/wiki/Geographic_distribution_of_Arabic#Population

[2] http://en.wikipedia.org/wiki/Big_data

Proceedings of the Second Workshop on Natural Language Processing for Social Media (SocialNLP), pages 22–27, Dublin, Ireland, August 24 2014.

Dialect identification is essential and considered the first prepossessing component for any natural language application dealing with Arabic and its variation such as machine translation, information retrieval for social media, sentiments analysis, opinion extraction, etc.

Herein, we present our effort on a part of the ASMAT project (*Arabic Social Media Analysis Tools*), which aims at creating tools for analyzing social media in Arabic. This project paves the way for end user targets (like machine translation and sentiment analysis) through pre-processing and normalization. There are, however, still many challenges to be faced.

This paper presents a first-step towards the ultimate goal of identifying and defining languages and dialects within the social media text. This paper is organized as follows: Section 2 presents related work. Sections 3 and 4 describe the probabilistic approach based on the character n-gram Markov language model and Naive Bayes classifier. Section 5 presents the data set, the several conducted experiments and their results. Conclusions and future work are presented in Section 6.

2 Related Work

There have been several works on Arabic Natural Language Processing (NLP). However, most traditional techniques have focused on MSA, since it is understood across a wide spectrum of audience in the Arab world and is widely used in the spoken and written media. Few works relate the processing of dialectal Arabic that is different from processing MSA. First, dialects leverage different subsets of MSA vocabulary, introduce different new vocabulary that are more based on the geographical location and culture, exhibit distinct grammatical rules, and adds new morphologies to the words. The gap between MSA and Arabic dialects has affected morphology, word order, and vocabulary (Kirchhoff and Vergyri, 2004). Almeman and Lee (2013) have shown in their work that only 10% of words (unigram) share between MSA and dialects.

Second, one of the challenges for Arabic NLP applications is the mixture usage of both AD and MSA within the same text in social media context. Recently, research groups have started focusing on dialects. For instance, Columbia University provides a morphological analyzer (MAGAED) for Levantine verbs and assumes the input is non-noisy and purely Levantine (Habash and Rambow, 2006).

Dialect Identification task has the same nature of language identification (LI) task. LI systems achieved high accuracy even with short texts (Baldwin and Lui, 2010), (Cavnar and Trenkle, 1994), (Joachims, 1998), (Kikui,1996); however, the challenge still exists when the document contains a mixture of different languages, which is actually the case for the task of dialect identification, where text is a mixture of MSA and dialects, and the dialects share a considerable amount of vocabularies. Biadsy and al. (2009) present a system that identifies dialectal words in speech and their dialect of origin through the acoustic signals. Salloum and Habash (2011) tackle the problem of AD to English Machine Translation (MT) by pivoting through MSA. The authors present a system that applies transfer rules from AD to MSA then uses state of the art MSA to English MT system. Habash and al. (2012) present CODA, a Conventional Orthography for Dialectal Arabic that aims to standardize the orthography of all the variants of AD while Dasigi and Diab (2011) present an unsupervised clustering approach to identify orthographic variants in AD.

Recently, Elfardy and Diab (Elfardy and al., 2013) introduced a supervised approach for performing sentence level dialect identification between Modern Standard Arabic and Egyptian Dialectal Arabic. The system achieved an accuracy of 85.5% on an Arabic online-commentary dataset outperforming a previously proposed approach achieving 80.9% and reflecting a significant gain over a majority baseline of 51.9% and two strong baseline systems of 78.5% and 80.4%, respectively (Elfardy and Diab, 2012).

Our proposed approach for dialect identification focuses on character-based n-gram Markov language models and Naive Bayes classifiers.

Character n-gram model is well suited for language identification and dialect identification tasks that have many languages and/or dialects, little training data and short test samples.

One of the main reasons to use a character-based model is that most of the variation between dialects, is based on affixation, which can be extracted easily by the language model, though also there are word-based features which can be detected by lexicons.

3 N-Gram Markov Language Model

There are two popular techniques for language identification. The first approach is based on popular words or stop-words for each language, which score the text based on these words (Gotti and al., 2013). The second approach is more statistical oriented. This approach is based on n-gram model (Cavnar and Trenkle, 1994), Hidden Markov model (Dunning, 1994) and support vector machine (Joachims, 1998).

A language model is one of the main components in many NLP tools and applications. Thus, lot of efforts have been spent for developing and improving features of the language models.

Our proposed approach uses the Markov model to calculate the probability that an input text is derived from a given language model built from training data (Dunning, 1994). This model enables the computation of the probability *P(S)* or likelihood, of a sentence *S*, by using the following chain formula in equation 1:

$$P(w_1,w_2,..., w_n) = P(w_1) \prod_{i=2}^{n} P(w_i|w_1... w_{i-1}) \qquad (1)$$

Where, the sequence $(w_1, ..., w_n)$ represents the sequence of characters in a sentence *S*. $P(w_i \mid w_1, ..., w_{i-1})$ represents the probability of the character w_i given the sequence $w_1, ..., w_{i-1}$.

Generally, the related approach that determines the probability of a word sequence is not very helpful because of its computational cost that is considered as very expensive.

Markov models assume that we can predict the probability of some future unit without looking too far into the past. So we could apply the Markov assumption to the above chain probability in Formula 1, by looking to zero character (uni-gram), one character (bi-gram), two characters (tri-gram).

The intuition behind using n-gram models in a dialect identification task is related to the variation in the affixations that are attached to words, which can be detected by bi-gram or tri-gram models.

4 Naïve Bayed Classifier

Naive Bayes classifier is a simple and effective probabilistic learning algorithm. A naive Bayes classifier is a simple probabilistic classifier based on applying Bayes' theorem with strong (naive) independence assumptions. A more descriptive term for the underlying probability model would be "independent feature model"[3].

In text classification, this classifier assigns the most likely category or class to a given document *d* from a set of pre-define N classes as $c_1, c_2, ..., c_N$. the classification function *f* maps a document to a category *(f: D ➔ C)* by maximizing the probability of the following equation (Peng and Schuurmans, 2003):

$$P(c|d) = \frac{P(c) \times P(d \mid c)}{P(d)} \qquad (7)$$

Where, *d* and *c* denote each the document and the category, respectively. In text classification a document *d* can be represented by a vector of *T attribute* $d=(t_1,t_2, ..., t_T)$.

Assuming that all attribute t_i are independent given the category *c*, then we can calculate $p(d|c)$ with the following equation:

$$\underset{c \in C}{\text{argmax}}\, P(c|d) = \underset{c \in C}{\text{argmax}}\, P(c) \times \prod_{i=1}^{T} P(t_i|c) \qquad (8)$$

The attribute term t_i can be a vocabulary term, local n-gram, word average length, or global syntactic and semantic properties (Peng and Schuurmans, 2003).

5 Experiments and Results

We have carried out two sets of experiments. The first set of experiments uses the character n-gram language model, while the second one uses the Naive Bayes classifier. The developed system identifies Arabic dialects using character n-gram models where the probability of each (Uni-gram, Bi-gram and Tri-gram) is calculated based on the training data within social media context.

---

[3]http://en.wikipedia.org/wiki/Naive_Bayes_classifier

5.1 Data

The System has been trained and tested using a data set collected from blogs and forums of different countries with Arabic as an official language. We have considered each regional language or dialect as belonging to one Arab country, although in reality a country most of the time may have several dialects. Moreover, there is a possible division of regional language within the six regional groups, as follows: Egyptian, Levantine, Gulf, Iraqi, Maghrebi and others (Zaidan and Callison-Burch, 2012). The different group divisions with their involved countries are defined as follows:

- *Egyptian:* Egypt;
- *Iraqi:* Iraq;
- *Gulf*: Bahrein, Emirates, Kuwait, Qatar, Oman and Saudi Arabia;
- Maghrebi: Algeria, Tunisia, Morocco, Libya, Mauritania;
- Levantine: Jordan, Lebanon, Palestine, Syria;
- Others: Sudan.

Moreover, there might be many other possible sub-divisions in one division, especially in the large region such as the Maghrebi. We used a data set that consists on the crowd source of social media texts such as forums and blogs. This set of data was manually collected and constructed using several (around eighteen) forums sites in Arabic. The collected texts were manually segmented to coherent sentences or paragraphs. For each dialect, sentences were saved in XML format with additional information such as sequence number, country, date, and the link. Table 1 shows some statistics about the collected text such as the total number of sentences or paragraph and number of words for each dialect. For each dialect 100 sentences were selected randomly for test purposes and were excluded from the training data. Moreover, statistics on the data set for each group of countries can be constructed, following the data set of Table 1.

Country	***#sentences***	***#words***
Egypt	7 203	72 784
Bahrain	3 536	36 006
Emirates	4 405	43 868
Kuwait	3 318	44 811
Oman	4 814	77 018
Qatar	2 524	22 112
Saudi Arabia	9 882	82 206
Jordon	1 944	18 046
Lebanon	3 569	26 455
Palestine	316	3 961
Syria	3 459	43 226
Algeria	731	10 378
Libya	370	5 300
Mauritania	2 793	62 694
Morocco	2 335	30 107
Tunisia	3 843	18 199
Iraq	1 042	13 675
Sudan	5 775	28 368

Table 1: Statistics about the dataset for each country

5.2 Results and Discussion

We have carried out three different experiments using uni-gram, bi-gram and tri-gram character for each experiment base on either the Markov language model or the Naive Bayes classifier. These different experiments show how character distribution (uni-gram) or the affixes of size 2 or 3 (bi-gram or tri-gram) help distinguish between Arabic dialects. The set of experiments were conducted on 18 dialects representing 18 countries. Furthermore, we conducted the experiments on six groups of Arabic dialects, which represent six areas as described in the earlier section.

For evaluation purposes, we considered the accuracy as a proportion of true identified test data and the *F*-Measure as a balanced mean between precision and recall. Our conducted experiments showed that the character-based uni-gram distribution helps the identification of two dialects, the Mauritanian and the Moroccan with an overall F-measure of 60% and an overall accuracy of 96%. Furthermore, the bi-gram distribution of two characters affix helps recognize four dialects, the Mauritanian, Moroccan, Tunisian and Qatari, with an overall F-measure of 70% and overall accuracy of 97%.

Last, the tri-gram distribution of three characters affix helps recognize four dialects, the Mauritanian, Tunisian, Qatari and Kuwaiti, with an overall F-measure of 73% and an overall accuracy of 98%. Our comparative results show that the character-based tri-gram and bi-gram distributions have performed better than the uni-gram distribution for most dialects. Overall, for eighteen dialects, the bi-gram model performed better than other models (uni-gram and tri-gram).

Since many dialects are related to a region, and these Arabic dialects are approximately similar, we also consider the accuracy of dialects group. Again, the bi-gram and tri-gram character Markov language model performed almost same, although the F-Measure of bi-gram model for all dialect groups is higher than tri-gram model except for the Egyptian dialect. Therefore, in average for all dialects, the character-based bi-gram language model performs better than the character-based uni-gram and tri-gram models.

Our results show that the Naive Bayes classifiers based on character uni-gram, bi-gram and tri-gram have better results than the previous character-based uni-gram, bi-gram and tri-gram Markov language models, respectively. An overall F-measure of 72% and an accuracy of 97% were noticed for the eighteen Arabic dialects. Furthermore, the Naive Bayes classifier that is based on a bi-gram model has an overall F-measure of 80% and an accuracy of 98%, except for the Palestinian dialect because of the small size of data. The Naive Bayes classifier based on the tri-gram model showed an overall F-measure of 78% and an accuracy of 98% except for the Palestinian and Bahrain dialects. This classifier could not distinguish between Bahrain and Emirati dialects because of the similarities on their three affixes. In addition, the naive Bayes classifier based on a character bi-gram performed better than the classifier based on a character tri-gram. Also, the accuracy of dialect groups for the Naive Bayes classifier based on character bi-gram model yielded better results than the two other models (uni-gram and tri-gram).

6 Conclusion

In this study, we presented a comparative study on dialect identification of Arabic language using social media texts; which is considered as a very hard and challenging task. We studied the impact of the character n-gram Markov models and the Naive Bayes classifiers using three n-gram models, uni-gram, bi-gram and tri-gram. Our results showed that the Naive Bayes classifier performs better than the character n-gram Markov model for most Arabic dialects. Furthermore, the Naive Bayes classifier based on character bi-gram model was more accurate than other classifiers that are based on character uni-gram and tri-gram. Last, our study showed that the six Arabic dialect groups could be distinguished using the Naive Bayes classifier based on character n-gram model with a very good performance.

As for future work, it would be interesting to explore the impact of the number of dialects or languages on a classifier. Also, it would be interesting to explore the influence of size of training and test set for both character n-gram Markov model and Naive Bayes classifier based on character n-gram model. We are planning to use more social media data from Twitter or Facebook in order to estimate the accuracy of these two models in the identification of the dialect and the language. Another extension to this work is to study a hybrid model for dialect identification involving character-based and word-based models. Finally, what we presented in this draft is a preliminary research on exploiting social media corpora for Arabic in order to analyze them and exploit them for NLP applications. Further extensions to this research include the translation of social media data to other languages and dialects, within the scope of the ASMAT project.

Reference

Al-Sabbagh R. and Girju R. 2013. Yadac : Yet another dialectal arabic corpus. In N. C. C. Chair, K. Choukri, T. Declerck, M. U. Doan, B. Maegaard, J. Mariani, J. Odijk, and S. Piperidis, editors, Proceedings of the Eight International Conference on Language Resources and Evaluation (LREC'12), Istanbul, Turkey, May 2012.

Almeman K. and Lee M. 2013. Automatic building of arabic multi dialect text corpora by bootstrapping dialect words. In Communications, Signal Processing, and their Applications (ICCSPA), 2013.

Baldwin T. and Lui M. 2010. Language identification: The long and the short of the matter. In Human Language Technologies: The 2010 Annual Conference of theNorth American Chapter of the Association for Computational Linguistics, HLT'10, pages 229{237, Stroudsburg, PA, USA, 2010. Association for Computational Linguistics.

Biadsy F., Hirschberg J., and Habash N. 2009. Spoken arabic dialect identification using phonotactic modeling. In Proceedings of the Workshop on Computational Approaches to Semitic Languages at the meeting of the European Association for Computational Linguistics (EACL), Athens, Greece.

Cavnar W. B., Trenkle J. M. 1994. N-gram-based text categorization. 1994. In Proceedings of SDAIR-94, 3rd Annual Symposium on Document Analysis and Information Retrieval. Ann Arbor MI, 48113(2):161{175, 1994.

Dasigi P. and Diab M. 2011. Codact: Towards identifying orthographic variants in dialectal arabic. In Proceedings of the 5th International Joint Conference on Natural Language Processing (ICJNLP), Chiangmai, Thailand, 2011.

Dunning T. 1994. Statistical identification of languages. Citeseer, 1994.

Elfardy H. and Diab M. 2012. Simplified guidelines for the creation of large scale dialectal arabic annotations. In Proceedings of the 8th International Conference on Language Resources and Evaluation (LREC), Istanbul, Turkey.

Elfardy H. and Diab M. 2013. Sentence-Level Dialect Identification in Arabic, In Proceedings of the 51st Annual Meeting of the Association for Computational Linguistics, ACL 2013, Sofia, Bulgaria. 2013.

Elfardy H., Al-Badrashiny M., Elfardy M. and Diab M. 2013. Sentence Level Dialect Identification in Arabic. In Proceedings of the 51st Annual Meeting of the Association for Computational Linguistics, pages 456–461, Sofia, Bulgaria, August 4-9 2013.

Gotti F., Langlais P., and Farzindar A. 2013. Translating government agencies' tweet feeds: Specificities, problems and (a few) solutions. In Proceedings of the Workshop on Language Analysis in Social Media, Atlanta, Georgia, June 2013. Association for Computational Linguistics, Association for Computational Linguistics.

Habash N. and Rambow O. 2006. MAGEAD: A morphological analyzer and generator for the Arabic dialects. In Proceedings of the 21st International Conference on Computational Linguistics and 44th Annual Meeting of the Association for Computational Linguistics , pages 681–688, Sydney, Australia, July. Association for Computational Linguistics.

Habash N., Diab M., and Rabmow O. 2012. Conventional orthography for dialectal arabic. In Proceedings of the Language Resources and Evaluation Conference (LREC), Istanbul, Turkey, 2012.

Joachims T. 1998. Text categorization with support vector machines: Learning with many relevant features. Springer, 1998.

Kikui G.-i. 1996. Identifying, the coding system and language, of on-line documents on the internet. In Proceedings of the 16th Conference on Computational Linguistics - Volume 2, COLING '96, pages 652{657, Stroudsburg, PA, USA, 1996. Association for Computational Linguistics.

Kirchhoff K. and Vergyri D. 2004. Cross-dialectal acoustic data sharing for arabic speech recognition. In Acoustics, Speech, and Signal Processing, 2004. Proceedings.(ICASSP'04). IEEE International Conference on, volume 1, pages I-765. IEEE, 2004.

Peng F. and Schuurmans D. 2003. Combining naive bayes and n-gram language models for text classi_cation. In Advances in Information Retrieval, pages 335{350. Springer, 2003.

Salloum W. and Habash N. 2011. Dialectal to standard arabic paraphrasing to improve arabic-english statistical machine translation. In Proceedings of the First Workshop on Algorithms and Resources for Modelling of Dialects and Language Varieties , pages 10–21. Association for Computational Linguistics.

Suliman A. F. 2008. Automatic Identification of Arabic Dialects USING Hidden Markov Models. Doctoral Dissertation, University of Pittsburgh. 2008.

Zaidan O. F. and Callison-Burch C. 2011. The arabic online commentary dataset: an annotated dataset of informal arabic with high dialectal content. In Proceedings of ACL, pages 37–41, 2011.

Zaidan O. F. and Callison-Burch C. 2012. Arabic dialect identi_cation. volume 1, Microsoft Research, 2012.

A Rule-Based Approach to Aspect Extraction from Product Reviews

Soujanya Poria
Dept of Computing Science & Maths
University of Stirling
soujanya.poria@cs.stir.ac.uk

Erik Cambria
School of Computer Engineering
Nanyang Technological University
cambria@ntu.edu.sg

Lun-Wei Ku
Institute of Information Science
Academia Sinica
lwku@iis.sinica.edu.tw

Chen Gui
SenticNet
chen@sentic.net

Alexander Gelbukh
Center for Computing Research
National Polytechnic Institute
gelbukh@cic.ipn.mx

Abstract

Sentiment analysis is a rapidly growing research field that has attracted both academia and industry because of the challenging research problems it poses and the potential benefits it can provide in many real life applications. Aspect-based opinion mining, in particular, is one of the fundamental challenges within this research field. In this work, we aim to solve the problem of aspect extraction from product reviews by proposing a novel rule-based approach that exploits common-sense knowledge and sentence dependency trees to detect both explicit and implicit aspects. Two popular review datasets were used for evaluating the system against state-of-the-art aspect extraction techniques, obtaining higher detection accuracy for both datasets.

1 Introduction

In opinion mining, different levels of granularity analysis have been proposed, each one having its own advantages and disadvantages. Aspect-based opinion mining (Hu and Liu, 2004; Ding et al., 2008) focuses on the extraction of aspects (or product features) from opinionated text and on the inference of polarity values associated with these. For example, a sentence like "I love the touchscreen of my phone but the battery life is so short" contains two aspects or opinion targets, namely *touchscreen* and *battery life*. In this case, applying a sentence level polarity detection technique would mistakenly result in a polarity value close to neutral, since the two opinions expressed by the users are opposite. Hence, aspect extraction is necessary to first deconstruct sentences into product features and then assign a separate polarity value to each of these features.

There are two types of aspects defined in aspect-based opinion mining: explicit and implicit. Explicit aspects are concepts that explicitly denote targets in the opinionated sentence. For instance, in the above example, *touchscreen* and *battery life* are explicit aspects as they are explicitly mentioned in the sentence. On the other hand, an aspect can also be expressed indirectly through an *implicit aspect clue* (IAC), e.g., in the sentence "This camera is sleek and very affordable", which implicitly provides a positive opinion about the aspects *appearance* and *price* of the entity *camera*.

Explicit aspect extraction has been widely researched and there exists several approaches for this task. Still, limited work has been done in extracting implicit aspects. This task is very difficult yet very important because the phenomenon of implicit aspects is present in nearly every opinionated document. For example, the following document extracted from the corpus (Hu and Liu, 2004) uses only implicit aspects:

Proceedings of the Second Workshop on Natural Language Processing for Social Media (SocialNLP), pages 28–37, Dublin, Ireland, August 24 2014.

> This is the best phone one could have. It has all the features one would need in a cellphone: It is lightweight, sleek and attractive. I found it very user-friendly and easy to manipulate; very convenient to scroll in menu etc.

Here, the word "lightweight" refers to the *weight* of the phone; the words "sleek" and "attractive" to its *appearance*; the compound "user-friendly" to its *interface*; the phrase "easy to manipulate" to its *functionality*; finally, the phrase "to scroll in menu" can be interpreted as a reference to the *interface* of the phone or its *menu*. Even though the aspects *appearance*, *weight* and *interface* do not appear in the sentence, the context contains clues that permit us to infer them. Namely, the words "sleek," "lightweight," and "user-friendly" that do occur in the context suggest these aspects.

In contrast to the task of identification of explicit aspects, the general scheme for identification of implicit aspects, a task called implicit aspect extraction, typically involves two steps:

1. Identify IACs (e.g., "sleek") in the opinionated document.

2. Map them to the corresponding aspects (e.g., *appearance*).

In this paper, we propose a novel approach to detect explicit aspects and IACs from opinionated documents. We also map IACs to their respective aspect categories. IACs are either single words, such as "sleek," or multi-word expressions, such as "easy to manipulate" as in the above example. Each IAC can be represented by a different part-of-speech (POS): in the example "This MP3 player is really expensive," the IAC "expensive" suggesting the aspect *price* is an adjective; in "This camera looks great," the IAC "look" suggesting *appearance* is a verb; in "I hate this phone. It only lasted less than six months!", the IAC "lasted" suggesting *durability* of the phone is a verb. In the following examples, IACs are nouns or noun phrases: "Even if I had paid full price I would have considered this phone a good deal," "Not to mention the sleekness of this phone", "The player keeps giving random errors", "This phone is a piece of crap."

In different contexts, the same implicit aspect can be implied by different IACs, as shown below for the implicit aspect *price*:

- This mp3 player is very affordable.
- This mp3 player also costs a lot less than the ipod.
- This mp3 player is quite cheap.
- This mp3 is inexpensive.
- I bought this mp3 for almost nothing!
- This mp3 player has been fairly innovative and reasonably priced.

A common approach for IAC identification is to assume that sentiments or polarity words are good candidates for IACs: for example, in "This MP3 player is really expensive," the word "expensive", which bears negative polarity, is also the IAC for the aspect *price*. However, this is not always true. For example, in "This camera looks great," the word "looks" implies the *appearance* of the phone, while polarity is conveyed through the word "great." In "I hate this phone. It only lasted less than six months!", the word "lasted" is the IAC for *durability* of the phone, while polarity is indicated by "hate." Furthermore, the second sentence of this example could appear without the first one: "This phone only lasted less than six months" and still constitute a negative opinion of the phone's *durability*, but not expressed by any specific word.

This phenomenon is known in opinion mining as *desirable fact*: communicating fact that by commonsense are good or bad, which indirectly implies polarity. For example, the objective fact "The camera can hold lots of pictures" does not contain any sentiment or polarity word yet gives a positive opinion about the camera's *memory capacity* (IAC "hold"), because it is desirable for a camera to hold many pictures.

In this paper, we present a rule-based approach that exploits common-sense knowledge and sentence dependency trees to detect both implicit and explicit aspects. In particular, the approach draws lessons from recent developments in common-sense reasoning (Cambria et al., 2011; Cambria et al., 2014a) and concept-level sentiment analysis (Xia et al., 2013; Poria et al., 2014) to first obtain the dependency structure of each sentence and, hence, exploit external knowledge to extract aspects and infer the polarity associated with them. The paper is organized as follows: Section 2 presents the literature in aspect extraction; Section 3 explains the features used for the labeler; Section 4 discusses novelty of the proposed methodology; Section 5 describes in detail the aspect extraction approach and results of the experimental evaluation; finally, Section 6 concludes the paper.

2 Related Work

Aspect extraction from opinionated text was first studied by Hu and Liu (Hu and Liu, 2004), who also introduced the distinction between explicit and implicit aspects. However, the authors only dealt with explicit aspects by adopting a set of rules based on statistical observations. Hu and Liu's method was improved by Popescu and Etzioni (Popescu and Etzioni, 2005) and by Blair-Goldensonh (Blair-Goldensohn et al., 2008). Popescu and Etzioni assumed the product class to be known as priori. Their algorithm detects whether a noun or noun phrase is a product feature or not by computing PMI between the noun phrase and the product class. Scaffidi et al. (Scaffidi et al., 2007) presented a method that uses a language model to identify product features. They assumed that product features are more frequent in product reviews than in general natural language text. However, their method seems to be very inaccurate in terms of precision as the retrieved aspects extracted by their method were very noisy.

Aspect extraction can be seen as a general information extraction problem, for which techniques based on *sequential labeling* are generally used. The most popular methods in this context, in particular, are *Hidden Markov Models* (HMM) and *Conditional Random Fields* (CRF) (Lafferty et al., 2001). Jin and Ho (Jin and Ho, 2009) used a lexicalized HMM for joint extraction of opinions along with their explicit aspects. Niklas and Gurevych (Niklas and Gurevych, 2010) used CRF to extract explicit aspects in a custom corpus with data of different domains. Li et al. (Li et al., 2010), Choi and Cardie (Choi and Cardie, 2010) and Huang et al. (Huang et al., 2012) also used CRF for extraction of explicit aspects.

As to the implicit aspects, the OPINE extraction system developed by Popescu and Etzioni (Popescu and Etzioni, 2005) was the first that leveraged on the extraction of this type of aspects to improve polarity classification. However, their system is not described in detail and is not publicly available. To the best of our knowledge, all existing methods for implicit aspect extraction are based on the use, in one or another way, of what we term IAC. Su (Su et al., 2008) proposed a clustering method to map IACs (which were assumed to be sentiment words) to their corresponding explicit aspects. The method exploits the mutual reinforcement relationship between an explicit aspect and a sentiment word forming a co-occurring pair in a sentence. Hai (Zhen et al., 2011) proposed a two-phase co-occurrence association rule mining approach to match implicit aspects (which were also assumed to be sentiment words) with explicit aspects. Finally, Zeng and Li (Zeng and Li, 2013) proposed a rule-based method to extract explicit aspects and mapped implicit features by using a set of sentiment words and by clustering explicit feature-word pairs.

3 Method

3.1 Corpus for aspect extraction

In order to evaluate the explicit aspect extraction algorithm, we use the corpus provided by (Hu and Liu, 2004) and the Semeval 2014 dataset[1] (Table 1). As for the implicit aspect extraction algorithm and lexicon, we use the corpus developed by Cruz-Garcia et al. (Cruz-Garcia et al., 2014), who manually labeled each IAC and their corresponding aspects in a well-known corpus for opinion mining (Hu and Liu, 2004). The corpus is publicly available for research purposes.[2]

[1] `http://alt.qcri.org/semeval2014/task4/index.php?id=data-and-tools`

[2] Available from `www.gelbukh.com/resources/implicit-aspect-extraction-corpus`, visited on March 19, 2014.

Table 1: Description of Semeval 2014 dataset

	Sentences Containing *n* aspect terms			
Domain Name	$n = 0$	$n \geq 1$	$n \geq 2$	total($n \geq 0$)
Restaurants	1,732	2,212	881	3,944
Laptops	1,883	2,065	456	3,948

3.2 Pre-Processing

Pre-processing is a key step for aspect parsing. The pre-processing module of the proposed framework consists of two major steps: firstly, the sentence dependency tree is obtained through *Stanford Dependency Parser*[3]; secondly, dependency structure elements are processed by means of *Stanford Lemmatizer* for each sentence. It is important to build the dependency tree before lemmatization as swapping the two steps results in several imprecisions caused by the lower grammatical accuracy of lemmatized sentences.

3.3 Aspect Parser

3.3.1 Implicit aspect lexicon

We use the implicit aspect corpus developed by Cruz-Garcia et al. (Cruz-Garcia et al., 2014), where IACs are indicated and manually labeled by their corresponding aspect categories. For our task, we extracted the sentences having implicit aspects and then extracted IACs for each of them, along with their corresponding labeled categories. For example, in "*The car is expensive*" the IAC is *expensive* and it is labeled by the category *price*. Below is the list of the aspect categories extracted from the corpus:

- functionality
- weight
- price
- appearance
- behavior
- performance
- quality
- service
- size

For each IAC under every aspect category, synonyms and antonyms were obtained from WordNet (Fellbaum, 1998) and stored under the same aspect category. For example, *expensive* and its antonym *inexpensive* both have the same category *price*. Semantics extracted from SenticNet (Cambria et al., 2014b) have also been exploited to enlarge the set of conceptually related IACs. Thus, a lexicon of 1,128 IACs categorized into the above categories was built.

3.3.2 Opinion Lexicon

We use SenticNet 3 as a concept-level opinion lexicon. The common-sense knowledge base contains 30,000 multi-word expressions labeled by their polarity scores. The proposed aspect parser is based on two general rules:

- Rules for the sentences having subject verb.
- Rules for the sentences which do not have subject verb.

[3]http://nlp.stanford.edu:8080/parser

A dependency relation is a binary relation characterized by the following features:

- The type of the relation that specifies the nature of the (syntactic) link between the two elements in the relation.
- The head of the relation: this is the element that is the pivot of the relation. Core syntactic and semantics properties (e.g., agreement) are inherited from the head.
- The dependent is the element that depends on the head and which usually inherits some of its characteristics (e.g., number, gender in the case of agreement).

Most of the times, the active token is considered in a relation if it acts as the head of the relation, although there are exceptions. Once the active token has been identified as the trigger for a rule, there are several ways to compute its contribution, depending on how the dependency relation and the properties of the tokens match with the rules. The preferred way is not to consider the contribution of the token alone, but in combination with the other elements in the dependency relation. First of all, Stanford parser is used to obtain the dependency parse structure of each sentence. Then, hand-crafted dependency rules are employed on the parse trees to extract aspects.

3.3.3 Subject Noun Rule

Trigger: when the active token is found to be the syntactic subject of a token. *Behavior:* if an active token h is in a subject noun relationship with a word t then:

1. if t has any adverbial or adjective modifier and the modifier exists in SenticNet, then t is extracted as an aspect.
2. if the sentence does not have auxiliary verb, i.e., *is, was, would, should, could*, then:
   - if the verb t is modified by an adjective or an adverb or it is in *adverbial clause modifier* relation with another token, then both h and t are extracted as aspects. In (1), *battery* is in a subject relation with *lasts* and *lasts* is modified by the adjective modifier *little*, hence both the aspects *last* and *battery* are extracted.

     (1) The battery lasts little.

   - if t has any direct object relation with a token n and the POS of the token is *Noun* and n is not in SenticNet, then n is extracted as an aspect. In (2), *like* is in direct object relation with *lens* so the aspect *lens* is extracted.

     (2) I like the lens of this camera.

   - if t has any direct object relation with a token n and the POS of the token n is *Noun* and n exists in SenticNet, then the token n extracted as aspect term. In the dependency parse tree of the sentence, if another token n_1 is connected to n using any dependency relation and the POS of n_1 is *Noun*, then n_1 is extracted as an aspect. In (3), *like* is in direct object relation with *beauty* which is connected to *screen* via a preposition relation. So the aspects *screen* and *beauty* are extracted.

     (3) I like the beauty of the screen.

   - if t is in open clausal complement relation with a token t_1, then the aspect t-t_1 is extracted if t-t_1 exists in the opinion lexicon. If t_1 is connected with a token t_2 whose POS is *Noun*, then t_2 is extracted as an aspect. In (4), *like* and *comment* is in clausal complement relation and *comment* is connected to *camera* using a preposition relation. Here, the POS of *camera* is *Noun* and, hence, *camera* is extracted as an aspect.

     (4) I would like to comment on the camera of this phone.

3. A copula is the relation between *the complement of a copular verb* and *the copular verb*. If the token t is in copula relation with a copular verb and the copular verb exists in the implicit aspect lexicon, then t is extract as aspect term. In (5), *expensive* is extracted as an aspect.

   (5) The car is expensive.

4. If the token t is in copula relation with a copular verb and the POS of h is *Noun*, then h is extracted as an explicit aspect. In (6), *camera* is extracted as an aspect.

   (6) The camera is nice.

5. If the token t is in copula relation with a copular verb and the copular verb is connected to a token t_1 using any dependency relation and t_1 is a verb, then both t_1 and t are extracted as implicit aspect terms, as long as they exist in the implicit aspect lexicon. In (7), *lightweight* is in copula relation with *is* and *lightweight* is connected to the word *carry* by open clausal complement relation. Here, both *lightweight* and *carry* are extracted as aspects.

   (7) The phone is very lightweight to carry.

3.3.4 Sentences which do not have subject noun relation in their parse tree

For sentences that do not have noun subject relation in their parse trees, aspects are extracted using the following rules:

1. if an adjective or adverb h is in infinitival or open clausal complement relation with a token t and h exists in the implicit aspect lexicon, then h is extracted as an aspect. In (8), *big* is extracted as an aspect as it is connected to *hold* using a clausal complement relation.

   (8) Very big to hold.

2. if a token h is connected to a noun t using a prepositional relation, then both h and t are extracted as aspects. In (9) *sleekness* is extracted as an aspect.

   (9) Love the sleekness of the player.

3. if a token h is in a direct object relation with a token t, t is extracted as aspect. In (10), *mention* is in a direct object relation with *price*, hence *price* is extracted as an aspect.

   (10) Not to mention the price of the phone.

3.3.5 Additional Rules

- For each aspect term extracted above, if an aspect term h is in co-ordination or conjunct relation with another token t, then t is also extracted as an aspect. In (11), *amazing* is firstly extracted as an aspect term. As *amazing* is in conjunct relation with *easy*, then *use* is also extracted as an aspect.

  (11) The camera is amazing and easy to use.

- A noun compound modifier of an NP is any noun that serves to modify the head noun. If t is extracted as an aspect and t has noun compound modifier h, then the aspect *h-t* is extracted and t is removed from the aspect list. In (12), as *chicken* and *casserole* are in *noun compound modifier* relation, only *chicken casserole* is extracted as an aspect.

  (12) We ordered the chicken casserole, but what we got were a few small pieces of chicken, all dark meat and on the bone.

4 Novelty of the proposed work

First of all, the proposed method is fully unsupervised and depends on the accuracy of the dependency parser and the opinion lexicon, rather then a training corpus and supervised learning accuracy. Only (Qiu et al., 2011) follow an unsupervised learning approach but the proposed method uses an enhanced set of rules and opinion lexicon. The proposed method also outperforms (Qiu et al., 2011) on the same dataset they used. Implicit aspects extracted through the proposed method differ from *implicit aspect expressions* defined by Liu (Liu, 2012) as "aspect expressions that are not nouns or noun phrases" in that implicit aspects extracted by the proposed algorithm semantically refer to the values of the pre-defined aspects, irrespective of their own surface POS. Below are listed some examples where the implicit aspect terms are either noun or noun phrases.
In (13), the IAC *deal* is extracted.

(13) Even if I had paid full price I would have considered this phone a good *deal*.

In (14), *sleekness* is extracted as an IAC.

(14) Not to mention the *sleekness of this phone*.

In (15), the IAC *errors* is extracted by the algorithm.

(15) The player keeps giving random *errors*.

In (16), *piece of crap* is a noun phrase and is extracted as an IAC by the proposed algorithm.

(16) This phone is a *piece of crap*.

A demo of the developed aspect parser is freely available at `http://sentic.net/demo`.

Table 2: Results on the DVD-player review dataset provided by (Hu and Liu, 2004)

Algorithm	Precision	Recall
Hu and Liu	75.00%	82.00%
Popescu and Etzioni	89.00%	80.00%
Dependency propagation method	87.00%	81.00%
Proposed approach	89.25%	91.25%

Table 3: Results on the Canon G3 review dataset provided by (Hu and Liu, 2004)

Algorithm	Precision	Recall
Hu and Liu	71.00%	79.00%
Popescu and Etzioni	87.00%	74.00%
Dependency propagation method	90.00%	81.00%
Proposed approach	90.15%	92.25%

Table 4: Results on the Jukebox review dataset provided by (Hu and Liu, 2004)

Algorithm	Precision	Recall
Hu and Liu	72.00%	76.00%
Popescu and Etzioni	89.00%	74.00%
Dependency propagation method	90.00%	86.00%
Proposed approach	92.25%	94.15%

Table 5: Results on the Nikon Coolpix review dataset provided by (Hu and Liu, 2004)

Algorithm	Precision	Recall
Hu and Liu	69.00%	82.00%
Popescu and Etzioni	86.00%	80.00%
Dependency propagation method	81.00%	84.00%
Proposed approach	82.15%	86.15%

Table 6: Results on the Nokia-6610 review dataset provided by (Hu and Liu, 2004)

Algorithm	Precision	Recall
Hu and Liu	74.00%	80.00%
Popescu and Etzioni	90.00%	78.00%
Dependency propagation method	92.00%	86.00%
Proposed approach	93.25%	93.32%

5 Experiments and Results

5.1 Experiment on the dataset provided by (Hu and Liu, 2004)

Experimental evaluation was carried out on the dataset derived from (Hu and Liu, 2004). As discussed in Section 3, the proposed method is able to extract both explicit and implicit aspects. To the best of our knowledge, there is no state-of-the-art benchmark to evaluate implicit aspect extraction.

We compare the proposed framework with those in Hu and Liu (Hu and Liu, 2004), Qiu et al. (Qiu et al., 2011), and Popescu and Etzioni (Popescu and Etzioni, 2005) (which only carried out explicit aspect extraction). Table 2, Table 3, Table 4, Table 5 and Table 6 show that the proposed framework outperforms all existing methods in terms of both precision and recall.

6 Conclusion

We have illustrated a method for extracting both explicit and implicit aspects from opinionated text. The proposed framework only leverages on common-sense knowledge and on the dependency structure of sentences and, hence, is unsupervised. As future work, we aim to discover more rules for aspect extraction. Another key future effort is to combine existing rules for complex aspect extraction. To obtain the aspect categories of IACs, we have developed an aspect knowledge base using WordNet and SenticNet. We will focus on extending the scalability of such knowledge base and on making it as much noise-free as possible.

6.1 Experiment on Semeval 2014 dataset

We also carried out experiments on Semeval 2014 aspect based sentiment analysis data obtained from `http://alt.qcri.org/semeval2014/task4/index.php?id=data-and-tools`. Results are shown in Table 7. We cannot perform a comparative evaluation of such experimental results as there is no state-of-art approach yet which used this dataset for the same kind of experiment. Overall, results show high accuracy.

Table 7: Results on the Semeval 2014 dataset

Domain	Precision	Recall
Laptop	82.15%	84.32%
Restaurants	85.21%	88.15%

References

Sasha Blair-Goldensohn, Kerry Hannan, Ryan McDonald, Tyler Neylon, George A. Reis, and Jeff Reynar. 2008. Building a sentiment summarizer for local service reviews. In *Proceedings of WWW-2008 workshop on NLP in the Information Explosion Era*, page 14.

Erik Cambria, Thomas Mazzocco, Amir Hussain, and Chris Eckl. 2011. Sentic medoids: Organizing affective common sense knowledge in a multi-dimensional vector space. In D Liu, H Zhang, M Polycarpou, C Alippi, and H He, editors, *Advances in Neural Networks*, volume 6677 of *Lecture Notes in Computer Science*, pages 601–610, Berlin. Springer-Verlag.

Erik Cambria, Paolo Gastaldo, Federica Bisio, and Rodolfo Zunino. 2014a. An ELM-based model for affective analogical reasoning. *Neurocomputing*.

Erik Cambria, Daniel Olsher, and Dheeraj Rajagopal. 2014b. SenticNet 3: A common and common-sense knowledge base for cognition-driven sentiment analysis. *AAAI*, pages 1515–1521.

Yejin Choi and Claire Cardie. 2010. Hierarchical sequential learning for extracting opinions and their attributes. In *Proceedings of Annual Meeting of the Association for Computational Linguistics (ACL-2010)*, pages 268–274.

Ivan Cruz-Garcia, Alexander Gelbukh, and Grigori Sidorov. 2014. Implicit aspect indicator extraction for aspect-based opinion mining. *submitted*.

Xiaowen Ding, Bing Liu, and Philip S. Yu. 2008. A holistic lexicon-based approach to opinion mining. In *Proceedings of First ACM International Conference on Web Search and Data Mining (WSDM-2008)*, pages 231–240, Stanford University, Stanford, California, USA, Feb.

Christiane Fellbaum. 1998. *WordNet: An Electronic Lexical Database (Language, Speech, and Communication)*. The MIT Press.

Minqing Hu and Bing Liu. 2004. Mining and summarizing customer reviews. In *Proceedings of the ACM SIGKDD International Conference on Knowledge Discovery & Data Mining*, pages 168–177, Aug.

Sheng Huang, Xinlan Liu, Xueping Peng, and Zhendong Niu. 2012. Fine-grained product features extraction and categorization in reviews opinion mining. In *Proceedings of the IEEE 12th International Conference on Data Mining Workshops*, pages 680–686.

Wei Jin and Hung Hay Ho. 2009. A novel lexicalized HMM-based learning framework for web opinion mining. In *Proceedings of International Conference on Machine Learning (ICML-2009)*, pages 465–472.

John Lafferty, Andrew McCallum, and Fernando C.N. Pereira. 2001. Conditional random fields: probabilistic models for segmenting and labeling sequence data. In *Proceedings of the 18th International Conference on Machine Learning*, pages 282–289. Morgan Kaufmann Publishers.

Fangtao Li, Chao Han, Minlie Huang, Xiaoyan Zhu, Ying-Ju Xia, Shu Zhang, and Hao Yu. 2010. Structure-aware review mining and summarization. In *Proceedings of the 23rd International Conference on Computational Linguistics (COLING-2010)*, pages 653–661.

Bing Liu. 2012. *Sentiment Analysis and Opinion Mining*. Morgan & Claypool Publishers.

Jakob Niklas and Iryna Gurevych. 2010. Extracting opinion targets in a single and cross-domain setting with conditional random fields. In *Proceedings of Conference on Empirical Methods in Natural Language Processing (EMNLP-2010)*, pages 1035–1045.

Ana-Maria Popescu and Oren Etzioni. 2005. Extracting product features and opinions from reviews. In *Proceedings of Conference on Empirical Methods in Natural Language Processing (EMNLP-2005)*, pages 3–28.

Soujanya Poria, Erik Cambria, Gregoire Winterstein, and Guang-Bin Huang. 2014. Sentic patterns: Dependency-based rules for concept-level sentiment analysis. *Knowledge-Based Systems*.

Guang Qiu, Bing Liu, Jiajun Bu, and Chun Chen. 2011. Opinion word expansion and target extraction through double propagation. *Computational linguistics*, 37(1):9–27.

Christopher Scaffidi, Kevin Bierhoff, Eric Chang, Mikhael Felker, Herman Ng, and Chun Jin. 2007. Red opal: product-feature scoring from reviews. In *Proceedings of the 8th ACM conference on Electronic commerce*, pages 182–191. ACM.

Qi Su, Xinying Xu, Honglei Guo, Zhili Guo, Xian Wu, Xiaoxun Zhang, Bin Swen, and Zhong Su. 2008. Hidden sentiment association in chinese web opinion mining. In *Proceedings of International Conference on World Wide Web (WWW-2008)*, pages 959–968.

Rui Xia, Chengqing Zong, Xuelei Hu, and Erik Cambria. 2013. Feature ensemble plus sample selection: A comprehensive approach to domain adaptation for sentiment classification. *IEEE Intelligent Systems*, 28(3):10–18.

Lingwei Zeng and Fang Li. 2013. A classification-based approach for implicit feature identification. In *Chinese Computational Linguistics and Natural Language Processing Based on Naturally Annotated Big Data. 12th China National Conference, CCL 2013 and First International Symposium, NLP-NABD 2013, Suzhou, China, October 10–12, 2013, Proceedings*, volume 8202 of *Lecture Notes in Computer Science*, pages 190–202.

Hai Zhen, Kuiyu Chang, and Jung-jae Kim. 2011. Implicit feature identification via co-occurrence association rule mining. In *Computational Linguistics and Intelligent Text Processing. 12th International Conference, CICLing 2011, Tokyo, Japan, February 20–26, 2011. Proceedings, Part I*, volume 6608 of *Lecture Notes in Computer Science*, pages 393–404.

Multi-Lingual Sentiment Analysis of Social Data Based on Emotion-Bearing Patterns

Carlos Argueta
National Tsing Hua University
No. 101, Section 2, Kuang-Fu Road
Hsinchu, Taiwan
kid.a.rgueta@gmail.com

Yi-Shin Chen
National Tsing Hua University
No. 101, Section 2, Kuang-Fu Road
Hsinchu, Taiwan
yishin@gmail.com

Abstract

Social networking sites have flooded the Internet with posts containing shared opinions, moods, and feelings. This has given rise to a new wave of research to develop algorithms for emotion detection and extraction on social data. As the desire to understand how people feel about certain events/objects across countries or regions grows, the need to analyze social data in different languages grows with it. However, the explosive nature of data generated around the world brings a challenge for sentiment-based information retrieval and analysis. In this paper, we propose a multilingual system with a computationally inexpensive approach to sentiment analysis of social data. The experiments demonstrate that our approach performs an effective multi-lingual sentiment analysis of microblog data with little more than a 100 emotion-bearing patterns.

1 Introduction

Web 2.0 and the rise of social networking platforms such as microblogs have brought new ways to share opinions in a global setting. Microblogging sites represent a new way to share information about everything, such as new products, places of interest or popular culture in some ways replacing traditional word-of-mouth communication. Those sites have become rich repositories of opinions from audiences diverse in culture, race, location, and language. They represent, for people and businesses, a potential opportunity to understand what the global community thinks about them, helping them to make better informed decisions when improving their image and products. They may also offer the general public a way to find useful information and opinions before purchasing a product or service.

Vast swathes of the global population have access to nearly the same products and services. For that reason, being aware of opinions from around the world, regardless of the languages, is no longer ambitious but necessary. Systems which are able to aggregate opinionated data in multiple languages could highlight a global trend around a target query. This is desirable as targets may have different impacts depending on the area. The possibilities are huge but the challenges are many. As in every major endeavor, it is necessary to start with the basics, such as language detection and sentiment analysis.

With the explosive nature of subjective data in the Web, several patterns analysis techniques such as the ones bye Yi et al. (2003) and Davidov et al. (2010) have been proposed to extract opinionated and emotion-bearing data. Most works have focused on English language, except the technique proposed in (Sascha Narr and Albayrak, 2012) which utilizes n-grams as language independent features to classify tweets by their polarity in 4 different languages. However, since this technique relies solely on frequency statistics, it would need large training datasets.

In this paper, we propose a language independent approach to emotion-bearing patterns retrieval in microblog data. Each extracted pattern and its related words can also be considered as n-grams, however, selected in a way that makes them more semantically related to the domain of sentiment and emotion analysis. The proposed multi-lingual framework consists of two stages: Filter and Refine approach. In the Filter stage, the language and a hint of the polarity of a microblog post are detected based on the

Proceedings of the Second Workshop on Natural Language Processing for Social Media (SocialNLP), pages 38–43,
Dublin, Ireland, August 24 2014.

n-gram classification approach. Our approach is different from the one proposed in (Sascha Narr and Albayrak, 2012) in that the n-grams are used at the character-level instead of the word-level.

In the Refine stage, language-independent emotion-bearing words and patterns (using an adaptation of extraction methods by Davidov and Rappoport (2006)) are employed. Our approach differs from the method of Davidov et al. (2010) in that we use words belonging to empirically defined psychological and structural categories (emotion, cognition, etc.)[1]. These words are used as seeds to restrict the features extracted to emotion bearing patterns and words.

Our experimental results show that our approach can extract relevant patterns. With only about 100 patterns employed of about 31,500 n-gram candidates, the approach presented in this paper outperforms a state-of-the-art classifier for the French language. These results validate the potential of the proposed technique.

2 Related Work

Patterns have been extensively used for many Information Retrieval tasks. Pantel and Pennacchiotti (2006) extract semantic relations using generic patterns (with broad coverage but low precision). The key assumption is that in very large corpora like the Web, correct instances generated by a generic pattern will be instantiated by some reliable patterns, where reliable patterns are patterns that have high precision but often very low recall. Wang et al. (2007) propose a topical n-gram (TNG) model that automatically determines unigram words and phrases based on context, and assigns a mixture of topics to both individual words and n-gram phrases. They present an Information Retrieval (IR) application with better performance on an ad-hoc retrieval task over a TREC collection. Davidov and Rappoport (2006) have proposed an approach to unsupervised discovery of word categories based on symmetric patterns. A symmetric pattern is one in which co-occurring words can potentially belong to the same semantic category.

With the speed at which subjective data is generated on the Web, and its potential usage, patterns have also been applied to extract opinionated data. Yi et al. (2003) use a Sentiment Pattern Database to match sentiment phrases related to a subject from online texts. The system was verified using online product review articles. Dave et al. (2003) tried statistical and linguistic substitutions to transform specific patterns into more general ones. They also used an algorithm based on suffix trees to determine substrings that provide optimal classification. The extracted features were applied to opinion extraction of product reviews. In their work, Davidov et al. (2010) use their pattern definition (Davidov and Rappoport, 2006) to identify diverse sentiment types in short microblog texts.

Most of the work with patterns for sentiment extraction has focused on English language. Although, a few studies have identified patterns as a tool for bridging the gap between languages. Cui et al. (2011) automatically extracted different types of word level patterns (denoted emotion tokens), and labeled their sentiment polarities with an unsupervised propagation algorithm. Sascha Narr and Albayrak (2012) utilized n-grams as language independent features to classify tweets by their polarity in 4 different languages.

The main drawback of features such as n-grams is that, to capture the semantics of a specific domain, they rely solely on frequency statistics. This impacts less when large training data is available, but can be a considerable disadvantage when the data is scarce. Another drawback of such features is the large number of n-grams that need to be included in the features set. Larger feature spaces have a big impact on the efficiency of systems.

3 Methodology

The objective of this work is to propose an effective multi-lingual emotion-bearing patterns extraction approach. To test the relevance of the extracted features, a multi-lingual sentiment analysis system for microblog data is defined. The proposed framework illustrated in Figure 1 consists of two stages: the *Filter stage* and the *Refine stage*. Given a set of microblog posts containing a query term, the Filter stage utilizing n-gram patterns first detects the language of all the microblog posts. Then it obtains the polarity

[1] See the study by James W. Pennebaker and Booth (2007) and Tausczik and Pennebaker (2010)

(negative, positive) by utilizing a classifier trained with n-gram features at the character level. The Refine stage utilizing symmetric patterns performs a finer analysis of the posts to classify the ones that the Filter stage left out. It utilizes extracted emotion-bearing patterns as described in Section 3.1 and related words as features.

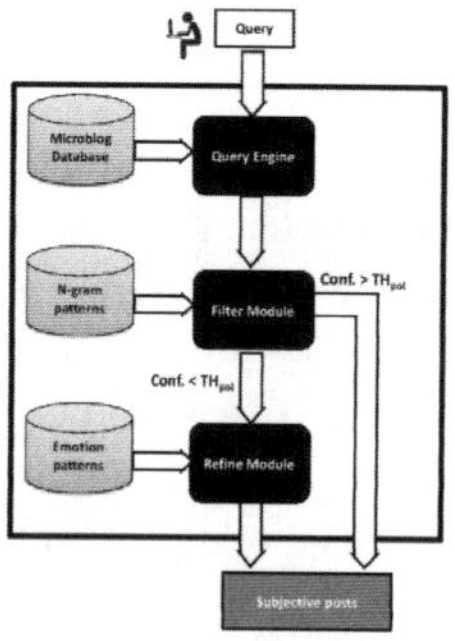

Figure 1: System Overview

3.1 Candidate Emotion-Bearing Surface Patterns Construction

The intuition of the construction method is based on psychological studies (James W. Pennebaker and Booth, 2007) proposing that emotional cues can be found in a person's utterances and texts, providing windows into their emotional and cognitive worlds. Based on this idea, the following method that can capture the textual emotion cues in the form of patterns and words is introduced.

The proposed extraction technique in this paper adapted the unsupervised word categories discovery technique introduced by Davidov and Rappoport (2006). To guarantee that the retrieved features are relevant to the sentiment analysis task here presented, the proposed emotion-bearing pattern extraction technique requires the following adaptations.

Other than the HW and CW word types introduced by Davidov and Rappoport (2006), the psychological word type (PW) is introduced as seeds for extracting more emotion-related patterns. Words in PW are content-bearing, and pertain to psychological categories related to emotion, cognition, affection, social, perception, etc. The PW set should include words like, "peace", "abandon", and "dream". By the symmetric nature of the patterns, the PW words can be naturally expanded from the extraction dataset . In order to drive the extraction towards more emotion-related patterns, it is also enforced that at least one of the CW words of a pattern contains a word from the PW set. For example, "peace is a dream" is an instance of a pattern "CW HW HW CW".

The result of the extraction is a large list of word subsequences related to different emotion-bearing patterns. There are two main reasons not to employ all extracted subsequences from a large corpus as features. First, the current list is usually huge (around 150,000 unique subsequences found in the experiments with English data), making the training process inefficient. Second, it is necessary to account for the fact that the dataset used for features extraction may be completely different from the training, and testing sets. Additionally, the PW set can also vary greatly in size and psychological categories included. This can potentially impact the coverage/accuracy due to unseen words.

3.2 Graph-Based Relevant Patterns Selection

The following reduction method based on the graph representation for patterns described in (Davidov and Rappoport, 2006) is introduced to reduce the features space, and to account for unseen words. First, infrequent subsequences are ignored. Then, the subsequences are grouped by pattern based on their HW words. Subsequences having the same HW word in the same positions are grouped together and their CW words are replaced by "*".[2] Finally, as proposed by Davidov and Rappoport (2006), the directed

[2] "*" is a wild card that matches any word

graph *G(p) = (V(G),E(G))* for each pattern p is constructed. For example, subsequences "love my niece" and "hate my boss" from the meta-pattern "CW HW CW" are both grouped together as part of the pattern "* my *".

Two different scores are proposed to measure the degree of emotion expressed by each pattern. The intuition of the following definitions is, the higher the proportion of PW words appearing in subsequences belonging to a given pattern, the higher the degree of emotion of this pattern.

Definition 1 *(SC1)*
The number of out-links of the vertex with max. number of out-links in the graph for pattern p.

$$SC1 = max(|\{(x, y)|x \in V(G(p)\}|) \quad (1)$$

Definition 2 *(SC2)*
The number of in-links of the vertex with max. number of in-links in the graph for pattern p.

$$SC2 = max(|\{(x, y)|y \in V(G(p)\}|) \quad (2)$$

Patterns with high SC1 and SC2 scores ensure a good coverage as they capture more PW words from the corpus. For each score, a ranked list of patterns is obtained. Patterns in top TH_{top} in at least one list and not in bottom TH_{bottom} in any list are retained. The final list of features is composed of all the retained patterns, and all the CWs it captured from the corpus through its related subsequences. This approach significantly reduces the features space by using only the relevant patterns, and not the subsequences (n-grams) as features. It also helps the coverage, as unseen words can still be captured by a pattern through the "* " wild card.

3.3 Multi-lingual Sentiment Analysis on Microblog Data

The following Filter and Refine approach is employed to determine the polarity of posts from microblog data. Given a post, the Filter stage firsts detects its language. It does so by training language models using n-grams at the character-level. Next, the corresponding polarity models are used to determine the polarity of the post. The polarity models are also constructed with the same method.

A confidence value is obtained as follows.

$$Conf(p) = \left|\sum(Freq_{positive}(ng) - Freq_{negative}(ng))\right| \quad (3)$$

where ng is an n-gram entry and *Freq* gets its frequency count in a polarity model.

We define experimentally two thresholds TH_{pol} for $pol \in \{positive, negative\}$. For a given detected class *pol* we say the post has that polarity only if *Conf(p)* $> TH_{pol}$ else we send the post to the Refine stage.

The posts not classified by the Filter stage are processed by the Refine stage, which is based on a Multinomial Naïve Bayes classifier. The classifier uses the emotion-patterns and words extracted using the methods described in 3.1 and 3.2 as binary features. Each pattern is used as a regular expression to look for matching subsequences in a post. If a match exists, the corresponding value in the vector is set to 1 and to 0 otherwise. The same process applies for word features.

4 Experiments

4.1 Experimental Setup

Two experiments were performed to validate the approach introduced in this paper. Datasets in three target languages (English, Spanish, and French) were utilized to test the approach. To avoid favoring the proposed method by having similar data characteristics in both training and testing stages, different datasets are employed in the experiments.

The larger set, Set_{HT}, was collected using emotion-bearing hashtags as noisy labels. This set is used during the training process. The second set, Set_{Emo}, was collected using positive and negative emoticons as queries to the Twitter Search API. From the collected tweets, 500 positive and 500 negative were manually annotated for each language by 2 volunteers. The third set Set_{RW}, released by Sascha Narr and Albayrak (2012), contains 739 positive and 488 negative manually annotated English tweets, and 159 positive and 160 negative French tweets.

To obtain more emotion-related patterns during the extraction phase, the psychological words (PW) were obtained from psychological categories in a text analysis application called Linguistic Inquiry and Word Count (LIWC) (James W. Pennebaker and Booth, 2007).

4.2 Experimental Result

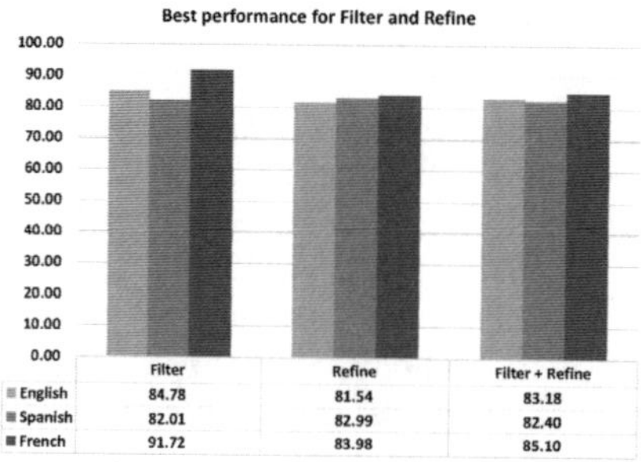

Figure 2: Filter + Refine performance with Set_{Emo} testing set

The first experiment evaluated the proposed approach using the Set_{Emo} testing set. The results in Figure 2 show that overall accuracies of over 80% can be obtained for all languages. Keep in mind that neither Filter nor Refine stages process all the posts, hence the reported individual accuracies are only over the portion of posts analyzed by each, with only the Filter+Refine result being over the totality of the posts. Due to time limitations, the approach used to combine the results from Filter and Refine is basic and treats both classifications as independent processes. A more elaborated approach may improve the results further.

Method	Lang	Patterns	Training Tweets	Accuracy
Narr	en	N.A.	≈ 500K	81.3 %
F+R	en	145	100K	79.0 %
Narr	fr	N.A.	≈ 100K	74.9 %
F+R	fr	100	50K	75.6 %

Table 1: Filter + Refine (F+R) compared to the related work (Narr).

Language	n-grams	patterns
English	141,981	145
Spanish	85,683	-
French	31,428	100

Table 2: Number of the extracted subsequences (n-grams), compared to the final number of patterns used in the comparison between Filter + Refine and Narr.

Finally, an experiment similar to the previous one was performed using Set_{RW} as the testing set. Table 1 shows that using a significantly lower number of features (the number of unigrams used by Narr is not available but must be large) and a smaller training set, the performance of the introduced approach surpasses the one reported by Narr for French and is just slightly lower for English. This is possible thanks to the effective reduction approach used to obtain relevant patterns from extracted subsequences, which is one of the main contributions of this paper (See Table 2). The training sizes used by Filter + Refine were limited due to data availability. More data would have probably helped Filter + Refine surpass the results reported by Narr for English.

5 Conclusion and Future Work

Two main types of language-independent features were studied in this paper: character-level n-grams, and emotion-bearing patterns. Character-level n-grams represent a useful tool for a preliminary sentiment classifier such as Filter. Emotion-bearing patterns can capture the emotional cues embedded in a person's writing. Such features can help identify subjectivity and determine the polarity of microblog posts across significantly different datasets in ways that regular patterns based purely on frequency wouldn't. It is believed that such emotion-bearing patterns can be used to perform a more complex analysis such as ambiguity and sarcasm identification, and to model other social and psychological characteristics of human behavior.

This paper contributes the introduction of emotion-bearing patterns as language independent features for multi-lingual sentiment analysis, and the efficient reduction approach used during their extraction. Sentiment analysis methods could benefit from such an approach during the training phases. Moreover, since the features obtained are very relevant to the classification task, less training examples are required, reducing the number of features significantly. Finally, the approach here presented is highly configurable, with both Filter and Refine relying on different thresholds. Several experiments with different sets of values can be performed to find the optimal set for a given language and show the full potential of the approach.

As a future work, it is planned to study the applicability of the presented approach to Asian languages such as Chinese and Vietnamese. Additionally, a deeper analysis of the patterns will be performed to extend the classification from the classic binary approach to a multi-class approach (using 8 different emotions). More difficult tasks such as detecting ambiguity and sarcasm will also be addressed.

References

Anqi Cui, Min Zhang, Yiqun Liu, and Shaoping Ma. 2011. Emotion tokens: bridging the gap among multilingual twitter sentiment analysis. In *Proceedings of the 7th Asia conference on Information Retrieval Technology*, AIRS'11, pages 238–249, Berlin, Heidelberg. Springer-Verlag.

Kushal Dave, Steve Lawrence, and David M. Pennock. 2003. Mining the peanut gallery: opinion extraction and semantic classification of product reviews. In *WWW '03: Proceedings of the 12th international conference on World Wide Web*, pages 519–528, New York, NY, USA. ACM.

Dmitry Davidov and Ari Rappoport. 2006. Efficient unsupervised discovery of word categories using symmetric patterns and high frequency words. In *Proceedings of the 21st International Conference on Computational Linguistics and the 44th annual meeting of the Association for Computational Linguistics*, ACL-44, pages 297–304, Stroudsburg, PA, USA. Association for Computational Linguistics.

Dmitry Davidov, Oren Tsur, and Ari Rappoport. 2010. Enhanced sentiment learning using twitter hashtags and smileys. In *Proceedings of the 23rd International Conference on Computational Linguistics: Posters*, COLING '10, pages 241–249, Stroudsburg, PA, USA. Association for Computational Linguistics.

Molly Ireland Amy Gonzales James W. Pennebaker, Cindy K. Chung and Roger J. Booth. 2007. The development and psychometric properties of liwc2007.

Patrick Pantel and Marco Pennacchiotti. 2006. Espresso: Leveraging generic patterns for automatically harvesting semantic relations. In *Proc. of the International Conference on Computational Linguistics/Association*, pages 113–120, Sydney, Australia, 17th-21st July. ACL Press.

Michael Hulfenhaus Sascha Narr and Sahin Albayrak. 2012. Language-independent twitter sentiment analysis. In *Workshop on Knowledge Discovery, Data Mining and Machine Learning*.

Yla R. Tausczik and James W. Pennebaker. 2010. The psychological meaning of words: Liwc and computerized text analysis methods.

Xuerui Wang, Andrew McCallum, and Xing Wei. 2007. Topical n-grams: Phrase and topic discovery, with an application to information retrieval. In *ICDM*, pages 697–702. IEEE Computer Society.

Jeonghee Yi, Tetsuya Nasukawa, Razvan Bunescu, and Wayne Niblack. 2003. Sentiment analyzer: Extracting sentiments about a given topic using natural language processing techniques. In *Proceedings of the IEEE International Conference on Data Mining (ICDM)*.

Recognition of Sentiment Sequences in Online Discussions

Victoria Bobicev
Technical University of Moldova
vika@rol.md

Marina Sokolova
University of Ottawa, Institute for Big Data Analytics, Canada
sokolova@uottawa.ca

Michael Oakes
Research Group in Computational Linguistics, University of Wolverhampton, UK
Michael.Oakes@wlv.ac.uk

Abstract

Currently 19%-28% of Internet users participate in online health discussions. In this work, we study sentiments expressed on online medical forums. As well as considering the predominant sentiments expressed in individual posts, we analyze sequences of sentiments in online discussions. Individual posts are classified into one of the five categories *encouragement, gratitude, confusion, facts,* and *endorsement.* 1438 messages from 130 threads were annotated manually by two annotators with a strong inter-annotator agreement (Fleiss kappa = 0.737 and 0.763 for posts in sequence and separate posts respectively). The annotated posts were used to analyse sentiments in consecutive posts. In automated sentiment classification, we applied HealthAffect, a domain-specific lexicon of affective words.

1 Introduction

Development of effective health care policies relies on the understanding of opinions expressed by the general public on major health issues. Successful vaccination during pandemics and the incorporation of healthy choices in everyday life style are examples of policies that require such understanding. As online media becomes the main medium for the posting and exchange of information, analysis of this online data can contribute to studies of the general public's opinions on health-related matters. Currently 19%-28% of Internet users participate in online health discussions (Balicco and Paganelli, 2011). Analysis of the information posted online contributes to effectiveness of decisions on public health (Paul and Drezde, 2011; Chee et al., 2009).

Our interest concentrates on sequences of sentiments in the forum discourse. It has been shown that sentiments expressed by a forum participant affect sentiments in messages written by other participants posted on the same discussion thread (Zafarani et al., 2010). Shared online emotions can improve personal well-being and empower patients in their battle against an illness (Malik and Coulson, 2010). We aimed to identify the most common sentiment pairs and triads and to observe their interactions. We applied our analysis to data gathered from the In Vitro Fertilization (IVF) medical forum.[1]

Below is an example of four consecutive messages from an embryo transfer discussion:

Alice: Jane - whats going on??

Jane: We have our appt. Wednesday!! EEE!!!

Beth: Good luck on your transfer! Grow embies grow!!!!

Jane: The transfer went well - my RE did it himself which was comforting. 2 embies (grade 1 but slow in development) so I am not holding my breath for a positive. This really was my worst cycle yet!!

In automated recognition of sentiments, we use HealthAffect, a domain-specific affective lexicon.

The paper is organized as follows: Section 2 presents related work in sentiment analysis, Section 3 introduces the data set and the annotation results, Section 4 presents HealthAffect, Section 5 describes the automated sentiment recognition experiments, and Section 6 discusses the results.

[1] http://ivf.ca/forums

Proceedings of the Second Workshop on Natural Language Processing for Social Media (SocialNLP), pages 44–49, Dublin, Ireland, August 24 2014.

2 Related Work

The availability of emotion-rich text has helped to promote studies of sentiments from a boutique science into the mainstream of Text Data Mining (TDM). The "sentiment analysis" query on Google Scholar returns about 16,800 hits in scholarly publications appearing since 2010. Sentiment analysis often connects its subjects with specific online media (e.g., sentiments on consumer goods are studied on Amazon.com). Health-related emotions are studied on Twitter (Chew and Eysenbach, 2010; Bobicev et al, 2012) and online public forums (Malik and Coulson, 2010; Goeuriot et al, 2012).

Reliable annotation is essential for a thorough analysis of text. Multiple annotations of topic-specific opinions in blogs were evaluated in Osman et al. (2010). Sokolova and Bobicev (2013) evaluated annotation agreement achieved on messages gathered from a medical forum. Bobicev et al. (2012) used multiple annotators to categorize tweets into positive, negative and neutral tweets. Merits of reader-centric and author-centric annotation models were discussed in (Balahur, Steinberger, 2009). In this work, we apply the reader-centric annotation model. We use Fleiss Kappa (Nichols et al, 2010) to evaluate inter-annotator agreement.

An accurate sentiment classification relies on electronic sources of semantic information. In (Sokolova and Bobicev, 2013; Goeuriot et al, 2011), the authors showed that the sentiment categories of SentiWordNet[2], WordNetAffect[3] and the Subjectivity lexicon[4] are not fully representative of health-related emotions. In the current work, we use HealthAffect, a domain-specific lexicon, to automatically classify sentiments. The lexicon has been introduced in (Sokolova and Bobicev, 2013).

Although there is a correlation between emotions expressed in consecutive posts (Chmiel et al, 2011; Tan et al, 2011; Hassan et al, 2012), so far health-related sentiment classification has focused on individual messages. Our current work goes beyond individual messages and studies sequences of sentiments in consecutive posts.

3 The IVF Data and Annotation Results

We worked with online messages posted on a medical forum. The forum communication model promotes messages which disclose the emotional state of the authors. We gathered data from the In Vitro Fertilization (IVF) website dedicated to reproductive technologies, a hotly debated issue in the modern society. Among the IVF six sub-forums, we selected the IVF Ages 35+ sub-forum[5] as it contained a manageable number of topics and messages, i.e., 510 topics and 16388 messages, where the messages had 128 words on average[6]. All topics were initiated by the forum participants. Among those, 340 topics contained < 10 posts. These short topics often contained one initial request and a couple of replies and were deemed too short to form a good discussion. We also excluded topics containing > 20 posts. This exclusion left 80 topics with an average of 17 messages per topic for a manual analysis by two annotators. First, we used 292 random posts to verify whether the messages were self-evident for sentiment annotation or required an additional context. The annotators reported that posts were long enough to convey emotions and in most cases there was no need for a wider context. We applied an annotation scheme which was successfully applied in (Sokolova and Bobicev, 2013).

We started with 35 sentiment types found by annotators and generalized them into three groups:

- ***confusion***, which included worry, concern, doubt, impatience, uncertainty, sadness, anger, embarrassment, hopelessness, dissatisfaction, and dislike;
- ***encouragement***, which included cheering, support, hope, happiness, enthusiasm, excitement, optimism;
- ***gratitude***, which included thankfulness.

A special group of sentiments was presented by expressions of compassion, sorrow, and pity. According to the WordNetAffect classification, these sentiments should be considered negative. However,

[2] http://sentiwordnet.isti.cnr.it/
[3] http://wndomains.fbk.eu/wnaffect.html
[4] http://mpqa.cs.pitt.edu/#subj_lexicon
[5] http://ivf.ca/forums/forum/166-ivf-ages-35/
[6] We harvested the data in July 2012.

in the context of health discussions, these emotional expressions appeared in conjunction with moral support and encouragement. Hence, we treated them as a part of *encouragement.* Posts presenting only factual information were marked as *facts*. Some posts contained factual information and strong emotional expressions; those expressions almost always conveyed encouragement (*"hope, this helps"*, *"I wish you all the best"*, *"good luck"*). Such posts were labeled *endorsement.* Note that the final categories did not manifest negative sentiments. In lieu of negative sentiments, we considered *confusion* as a non-positive label. *Encouragement* and *gratitude* were considered positive labels, *facts* and *endorsement* - neutral. It should be mentioned that the posts were usually long enough to express several sentiments. However, annotators were requested to mark messages with one sentiment category.

The posts that both annotators labelled with the same label were assigned to this category; 1256 posts were assigned with a class label. The posts labelled with two different sentiment labels were marked as *ambiguous*; 182 posts were marked as *ambiguous.*

Despite the challenging data, we obtained Fleiss Kappa = 0.737 which indicated a strong agreement between annotators (Osman et al, 2010). This value was obtained on 80 annotated topics. Agreement for the randomly extracted posts was calculated separately in order to verify whether annotation of separate posts was no more difficult than annotation of the post sequences. Contrary to our expectations, the obtained Fleiss Kappa = 0.763 was slightly higher than on the posts in discussions. The final distribution of posts among sentiment classes is presented in Table 2.

Classification category	Num of posts	Per-cent
Facts	494	34.4%
Encouragement	333	23.2%
Endorsement	166	11.5%
Confusion	146	10.2%
Gratitude	131	9.1%
Ambiguous	168	11.7%
Total	1438	100%

Table 2: Class distribution of the IVF posts.

We computed the distribution of sentiment pairs and triads in consecutive posts. We found that the most frequent sequences consisted mostly of *facts* and/or *encouragement*: 39.5% in total. *Confusion* was far less frequent and was followed by *facts* and *encouragement* in 80% of cases. That sentiment transition shows a high level of support among the forum participants. Approximately 10% of sentiment pairs are *factual* and/or *encouragement* followed by *gratitude*. Other less frequent sequences appear when a new participant added her post in the flow. Tables 3 and 4 list the results.

Sentiment pairs	Occurrence	Percent
facts, facts	170	19.5%
encouragement, encouragement	119	13.7%
facts, encouragement	55	6.3%
endorsement, facts	53	6.1%
encouragement, facts	44	5.1%

Table 3: The most frequent sequences of two sentiments and their occurrence in the data.

Sentiment triads	Occurrence	Percent
factual, factual, factual	94	12.8%
encouragement, encouragement, encouragement	63	8.6%
encouragement, gratitude, encouragement	18	2.4%
factual, endorsement, factual	18	2.4%
confusion, factual, factual	17	2.3%

Table 4: The most frequent triads of sentiments and their occurrences in the data.

4 HealthAffect

General affective lexicons were shown to be ineffective in sentiment classification of health related messages. To build a domain-specific lexicon, named HealthAffect, we adapted the Pointwise Mutual Information (PMI) approach (Turney, 2002). The initial candidates consisted of unigrams, bigrams and trigrams of words with frequency ≥ 5 appearing in unambiguously annotated posts (i.e., we omitted posts marked as uncertain). For each class and each candidate, we calculated PMI(*candidate, class*) as

$$\text{PMI}(candidate, class) = \log_2(\ p(candidate \text{ in } class)/(\ p(candidate)\ p(class))).$$

Next, we calculated Semantic Orientation (SO) for each candidate and for each class as

$$\text{SO}\ (candidate, class) = \text{PMI}(candidate, class) - \Sigma\ \text{PMI}(candidate, other\_classes)$$

where *other_classes* include all the classes except the class that Semantic Orientation is calculated for. After all the possible SO were computed, each HealthAffect candidate was assigned with the class that corresponded to its maximum SO.

Domain-specific lexicons can be prone to data over-fitting (since, for example, they might contain personal and brand names). To avoid the over-fitting pitfall, we manually reviewed and filtered out non-relevant elements, such as personal and brand names, geolocations, dates, stop-words and their combinations (since_then, that_was_the, to_do_it, so_you). Table 5 presents the lexicon profile. Note that we do not report the *endorsement* profile as it combines *facts* and *encouragement.*

Class	unigrams	bigrams	trigrams	total	Examples
Facts	204	254	78	536	`round_of_ivf, hearbeat, a_protocol`
Encourage-ment	127	107	68	302	`congratula-tions, is_hard, only_have_one`
Confusion	63	143	34	240	`crying, away_from, any_of_you`
Gratitude	37	51	34	122	`appreciate, a_huge, thanks_for_your`

Table 5: Statistics of the HealthAffect lexicon.

5 Sentiment Recognition

Our task was to assess HealthAffect's ability to recognise sentiments of health-related messages. We used the sentiment categories described in Section 3. In the experiments, we represented the messages by the HealthAffect terms. There were 1200 distinct terms, and each term was assigned to one sentiment.

Our algorithm was straightforward: it calculated the number of HealthAffect terms from each category in the post and classified the post in the category for which the maximal number of terms was found. Table 5 demonstrates that the number of terms was quite different for each category. Hence, the algorithm tended to attribute posts to the classes with a larger numbers of terms. To overcome the bias, we normalised the number of the terms in the post by the total number of terms for each category. The algorithm's performance was evaluated through two multiclass classification results:

- 4-class classification where all 1269 unambiguous posts are classified into (*encouragement, gratitude, confusion*, and neutral, i.e., *facts* and *endorsement*), and
- 3-class classification (positive: *encouragement, gratitude;* negative: *confusion*, neutral: *facts* and *endorsement*).

We computed micro- and macro-average *Precision (Pr), Recall (R) and F-score (F)* (Table 6).

Metrics	4-class classification	3-class classification
microaverage F-score	0.633	0.672
macroaverage Precision	0.593	0.625
macroaverage Recall	0.686	0.679
macroaverage F-score	0.636	0.651

Table 6: Results of 4-class and 3-class classification.

For additional assessment of HealthAffect, we ran simple Machine Learning experiments using Naïve Bayes and representing the texts through the lexicon terms. The obtained results of F-score=0.44, Precision=0.49, Recall=0.47 supported our decision to use HealthAffect in the straight-forward manner as presented above. For each sentiment class, our results were as follows:

- The most accurate classification occurred for *gratitude*. It was correctly classified in 83.6% of its occurrences. It was most commonly misclassified as *encouragement* (9.7%). Posts classified as *gratitude* are mostly the shortest ones containing only some words of gratitude and appreciation of others' help. As they usually do not contain any more information than this, there were fewer chances for them to be misclassified.
- The second most accurate result was achieved for *encouragement.* It was correctly classified in 76.7% of cases. It was misclassified as neutral (9.8%) because the latter posts contained some encouraging with the purpose of cheering up the interlocutor.
- The least often correctly classified class was neutral (50.8%). One possible explanation is the presence of the sentiment bearing words in the description of facts in a post which is in general objective and which was marked as factual by the annotators.

Recall from Section 3, that we consider *encouragement* and *gratitude* to be positive sentiments and *confusion* to be a negative one. The reported results show that positive sentiments were most misclassified within the same group or with neutral, e.g., *encouragement* was misclassified more as neutral or *gratitude* than as *confusion*, *gratitude* - more as *encouragement* or neutral than as *confusion.* On the other hand, *confusion* and negative sentiments were most often misclassified as neutral.

6 Discussion and Future Work

We have presented results of sentiment recognition in messages posted on a medical forum. Sentiment analysis of online medical discussions differs considerably from polarity studies of consumer-written product reviews, financial blogs and political discussions. While in many cases positive and negative sentiment categories are powerful enough, such a dichotomy is not sufficient for medical forums. We formulate our medical sentiment analysis as a multi-class classification problem in which posts were classified into *encouragement, gratitude, confusion, facts* and *endorsement*.

In spite of sentiment annotation being highly subjective, we obtained a strong inter-annotator agreement between two independent annotators (i.e., Fleiss Kappa = 0.73 for posts in discussions and Fleiss Kappa = 0.76 for separate posts). The Kappa values demonstrated an adequate selection of classes of sentiments and appropriate annotation guidelines. However, many posts contained more than one sentiment in most cases mixed with some factual information. The possible solutions in this case would be (a) to allow multiple annotations for each post; (b) to annotate every sentence of the posts.

A specific set of sentiments on the IVF forum did not support the use of general affective lexicons in automated sentiment recognition. Instead we applied the PMI approach to build a domain-specific lexicon HealthAffect and then manually reviewed and generalized it.

In our current work we went beyond analysis of individual messages: we analyzed their sequences in order to reveal patterns of sentiment interaction. Manual analysis of a sample of data showed that topics contained a coherent discourse. Some unexpected shifts in the discourse flow were introduced by a new participant joining the discussion. In future work, we may include the post's author information in the sentiment interaction analysis. The information is also important for analysis of influence, when one participant is answering directly to another one citing in many cases the post which she answered to.

We plan to use the results obtained in this study for analysis of discussions related to other highly debated health care policies. One future possibility is to construct a Markov model for the sentiment sequences. However, in any online discussion there are random shifts and alternations in discourse which complicate application of the Markov model.

In the future, we aim to annotate more text, enhance and refine HealthAffect, and use it to achieve reliable automated sentiment recognition across a spectrum of health-related issues.

References

Balicco, L., C. Paganelli. 2011. *Access to health information: going from professional to public practices*, Information Systems and Economic Intelligence: 4th International Conference - SIIE'2011.

Bobicev, V., M, Sokolova, Y. Jaffer, D. Schramm. 2012. *Learning Sentiments from Tweets with Personal Health Information.* Proceedings of Canadian AI 2012, p.p. 37–48, Springer.

Chee, B., R. Berlin, B. Schatz. 2009. *Measuring Population Health Using Personal Health Messages*. Proceedings of AMIA Symposium, 92 - 96.

Chew, C. and G. Eysenbach. 2010. *Pandemics in the Age of Twitter: Content Analysis of Tweets during the 2009 H1N1 Outbreak*. PLoS One, 5(11).

Chmiel, A., J. Sienkiewicz, M. Thelwall, G. Paltoglou, K. Buckley, A. Kappas, J. Holyst. 2011. *Collective Emotions Online and Their Influence on Community Life*. PLoS one.

Goeuriot, L., J. Na, W. Kyaing, C. Khoo,Y. Chang, Y. Theng and J. Kim. 2012. *Sentiment lexicons for health-related opinion mining*. Proceedings of the 2nd ACM SIGHIT International Health Informatics Symposium, p.p. 219 – 225, ACM.

Hassan, A., A. Abu-Jbara, D. Radev. 2012. *Detecting subgroups in online discussions by modeling positive and negative relations among participants*. In Proceedings of the 2012 Joint Conference on Empirical Methods in Natural Language Processing and Computational Natural Language Learning (pp. 59-70).

Malik S. and N. Coulson. 2010. *Coping with infertility online: an examination of self-help mechanisms in an online infertility support group.* Patient Educ Couns, vol. 81, no. 2, pp. 315–318

Nichols, T., P. Wisner, G. Cripe, and L. Gulabchand. 2010. *Putting the Kappa Statistic to Use.* Qual Assur Journal, 13, p.p. 57-61.

Osman, D., J. Yearwood, P. Vamplew. 2010. *Automated opinion detection: Implications of the level of agreement between human raters.* Information Processing and Management, 46, 331-342.

Paul, M. and M. Dredze. 2011. *You Are What You Tweet: Analyzing Twitter for Public Health.* Proceedings of ICWSM.

Sokolova, M. and V. Bobicev. 2013. *What Sentiments Can Be Found in Medical Forums*? Recent Advances in Natural Language Processing, 633-639

Tan, C., L. Lee , J. Tang , L. Jiang , M. Zhou, P. Li, 2011. *User-level sentiment analysis incorporating social networks*, Proceedings of the 17th ACM SIGKDD international conference on KDDM.

Turney, P.D. 2002. *Thumbs up or thumbs down? Semantic orientation applied to unsupervised classification of reviews*. Proceedings of ACL'02, Philadelphia, Pennsylvania, pp. 417-424.

Zafarani, R., W. Cole, and H. Liu. 2010. *Sentiment Propagation in Social Networks: A Case Study in LiveJournal.* Advances in Social Computing (SBP 2010), pp. 413–420, Springer.

Verbal Behaviors and Persuasiveness in Online Multimedia Content

Moitreya Chatterjee, Sunghyun Park*, Han Suk Shim*,
Kenji Sagae and **Louis-Philippe Morency**
USC Institute for Creative Technologies
Los Angeles, CA 90094
metro.smiles@gmail.com,
{ park, hshim, sagae, morency }@ict.usc.edu

Abstract

Persuasive communication is an essential component of our daily lives, whether it is negotiating, reviewing a product, or campaigning for the acceptance of a point of view. With the rapid expansion of social media websites such as YouTube, Vimeo and ExpoTV, it is becoming ever more important and useful to understand persuasiveness in social multimedia content. In this paper we present a novel analysis of verbal behavior, based on lexical usage and paraverbal markers of hesitation, in the context of predicting persuasiveness in online multimedia content. Toward the end goal of predicting perceived persuasion, this work also explores the potential differences in verbal behavior of people expressing a positive opinion (e.g., a positive movie review) versus a negative one. The analysis is performed on a multimedia corpus of 1,000 movie review videos annotated for persuasiveness. Our results show that verbal behavior can be a significant predictor of persuasiveness in such online multimedia content.

1 Introduction

A message that is "intended to shape, reinforce or change the responses of another or others" is categorized as *persuasive communication* (Miller, 1980), and it is particularly important for the role it plays in creating social influence and altering other people's opinions (Reardon, 1991; Zimbardo and Leippe, 1991). For instance, a persuasive advertisement could be a potential profit churner.

The growth of social networking sites on the Internet has resulted in an explosion of online content with the purpose of delivering persuasive messages. Websites such as YouTube, Vimeo and ExpoTV are examples of online media in which these messages propagate mainly in the form of videos. ExpoTV, in particular, is a repository of a large number of videos dedicated for product reviews in which people try to convince others in favor of or against the use of various products. This raises an interesting research problem as to what it is that makes certain speakers have a substantial impact on others' opinions while other speakers are ignored.

In this paper, we present a novel analysis of spoken persuasion in online multimedia content. Our work is motivated by prior research findings in psychology indicating that verbal behavior is a promising indicator for persuasive communication (Chaiken and Eagly, 1979; Werner, 1982). Such prior findings allow us to hypothesize that two primary types of verbal features will be predictive of persuasion: lexical features and paraverbal markers of hesitation. Additionally we explore the relationship of the sentiment of the content and perceived persuasion, by hypothesizing that speakers' exhibit different verbal behavior when expressing a positive opinion versus a negative one and taking into account these differences will improve prediction performance. We conduct several experiments in order to validate these hypotheses using a multimedia corpus of 1,000 movie review videos obtained from ExpoTV.com, which is a great source of online reviews. Our experiments followed by a detailed analysis also reveal a set of predictive features which characterize persuasive online presentations.

In the following section, we present an overview of related work. Section 3 elaborates on our re-

* Both authors contributed equally to this work.

Proceedings of the Second Workshop on Natural Language Processing for Social Media (SocialNLP), pages 50–58,
Dublin, Ireland, August 24 2014.

search hypotheses. In Section 4, we present our multimedia corpus. The details of the experiments with computational descriptors and methodology are described in Section 5. We discuss the results and findings in Section 6, and finally we conclude our paper and present some future directions of research in Section 7.

2 Related Work

Content in the form of written text are omnipresent in our society. Starting from books, magazines and newspapers to the now prevalent emails and blog posts, text-based content are an invaluable component for effective communication. Prior research reports possibly greater persuasiveness in written messages compared to visual or acoustic modalities in certain situations (Chaiken and Eagly, 1979; Werner, 1982). Past research has also revealed that for sophisticated messages, such as those used in a martial setting, written messages are more persuasive (Chaiken and Eagly, 1979).

Although the importance of studying verbal behavior for determining persuasiveness has been underscored in prior work in the field of communication sciences (O'Keefe, 2002) and this line of research gives us useful pointers to the factors that contribute to persuasiveness in text or verbal communication, they present no computational aspect, which is where we put our emphasis in the paper.

In the field of natural language processing, text classification based on bag-of-words has been a long standing approach (Lewis and Gale, 1994; Mitchell, 1997; Dave et al., 2003). In fact, Young et al. (2011) have explored lexical features in the specific context of predicting persuasion, but they focus their attention on studying persuasion in dialogue. Our work draws inspiration from such approaches but explores it in the specific context of predicting persuasiveness in online multimedia content using lexical and paraverbal features.

3 Research Hypotheses

Motivated by prior works and theoretical background, we designed our experiments to validate three hypotheses.

Since multiple prior works point to the usefulness of the text modality in persuasive communication and also to the power of text classification with lexical features in various tasks, we explored the feasibility of capturing the difference in verbal behavior between persuasive and unpersuasive expressions of opinions in online social multimedia content (specifically, movie reviews). The following is the hypothesis that we specifically tested with our experiments:

Hypothesis 1: Verbal behavior, as captured by lexical usage, is indicative of persuasiveness in online social multimedia content, irrespective of whether the opinion expressed is positive or negative.

Paraverbal behaviors indicative of hesitation can constitute important information for predicting persuasiveness. For instance, a speaker's stuttering or breaking his/her speech with filled pauses (such as *um* and *uh*) has influence on how other people perceive his/her persuasiveness. Although previous work (DeVault et al, 2013) suggests paraverbal behavior may be indicative of depression, another work on emotion prediction however, (Devillers et al., 2006) raised questions about its predictive power when compared to using standard cues derived from lexical usage. This leads us to our second hypothesis on paraverbal behaviors in the context of predicting persuasiveness:

Hypothesis 2: Paraverbal behaviors related to hesitation are indicative of persuasiveness in online social multimedia content.

Past research highlights the importance of the knowledge of the affective state of a document towards its perceived persuasiveness (Murphy, 2001). We therefore hypothesize the following:

Hypothesis 3: Knowledge of the sentiment polarity of a movie review improves classification of the speaker's perceived persuasiveness.

4 Dataset

ExpoTV.com is a popular website housing videos of product reviews. Each product review has a video of a speaker talking about a particular product as well as the speaker's direct rating of the product on an integral scale from 1 star (for most negative review) to 5 stars (for most positive review). This direct rating is useful for the purpose of our study because this allows us to study perceived persuasion under different directions of persuasion (in favor of or against). For instance, the speaker in a 5-

star movie review video would most likely try to persuade his/her audience in favor of watching the movie while the speaker in a 1-star movie review video would argue against watching the movie. We therefore collected a total of 1,000 movie review videos that were either highly positive or negative. The dataset consists of the following:

- **Positive Reviews**: 500 movie review videos with 5-star rating (315 males and 185 females).
- **Negative Reviews**: 500 movie review videos with 1 or 2-star rating, consisting of 216 1-star videos (151 males and 65 females) and 284 2-star videos (212 males and 72 females). We included 2-star videos due to the lack of enough 1-star videos on the website.

Each video in the corpus has a frontal view of one person talking about a particular movie, and the average length of the videos is about 94 seconds. The corpus contains 372 unique speakers and 600 unique movie titles and is available to the community for purposes of academic research[1].

4.1 Evaluation of Persuasiveness

Amazon Mechanical Turk (AMT), which is a popular online crowdsourcing platform, was used to obtain subjective evaluation of each speaker's perceived persuasiveness, following a similar annotation scheme as (Mohammadi et al., 2013). For each video in the corpus, we obtained 3 repeated evaluations on the level of persuasiveness of the speaker by asking the workers to give direct rating on each speaker's persuasiveness on a Likert scale from 1 (very unpersuasive) to 7 (very persuasive). A total of 50 native English-speaking workers based in the United States participated in the evaluation process online, and the task was evenly distributed among the 50 workers. To minimize gender influence, the task was distributed such that the workers only evaluated speakers of the same gender. The correlation between the mean score of every movie and the individual ratings was found to be 0.7 on the average (Pearson's Correlation Coefficient).

Once the evaluation was complete, we used the mean persuasiveness score for each video as the ground-truth measure of the speaker's perceived persuasiveness. In this initial effort, we focused on videos that were extremely persuasive or not persuasive at all. Hence, videos with a mean score of equal to or greater than 5.5 were taken as persuasive while those with a mean score of equal to or less than 2.5 were taken as unpersuasive. After this, we ended up with a total of 300 videos, specifically 157 videos of positive reviews (75 persuasive and 82 unpersuasive) and 143 videos of negative reviews (62 persuasive and 81 unpersuasive).

4.2 Transcriptions

Using AMT and 18 participants from the same worker pool for persuasiveness evaluation, we obtained verbatim transcriptions of these filtered 300 videos, including transcriptions for filled pauses and stutters. Each transcription was reviewed and edited by multiple in-house experienced transcribers for accuracy. We do not use automatic speech recognition techniques in order to avoid noisy transcriptions.

5 Experiments

In this section, we give details on the design of our computational descriptors followed by the experimental methodology.

5.1 Computational Descriptors

In our experiments, our main focus was on devising computational descriptors for verbal behaviors in terms of lexical usage and also in terms of paraverbal markers of hesitation that can capture indications of persuasiveness of the speaker.

Verbal (Lexical) Descriptors: As in many text classification tasks, we designed our verbal descriptors based on the bag-of-words representation using term frequency of both unigrams and bi-

[1] Dataset available online: http://multicomp.ict.usc.edu/

grams. Using the 300 filtered videos (see Section 4.1) and without feature selection, the numbers of unigrams reach around 4,500 and bigrams around 24,000. We did not proceed further with higher order n-grams because empirical evidence has shown that trigrams and other higher order n-grams do not always show improvement because they introduce problems related to the sparsity of features (Dave et al., 2003).

Paraverbal Descriptors of Hesitation: From the verbatim transcriptions of our corpus, we observed a set of frequent paraverbal cues that could potentially be associated with the level of persuasiveness. The set of descriptors is inspired from the findings of DeVault et al. (2013), who explored a similar set of generic paraverbal features in an interactive dialogue setting. However, we are interested specifically in the ones that capture signs of hesitation. The following were the descriptors that were used:

- **Pause-Fillers:** The verbal behaviors of reviewers are often characterized with various pause-fillers, such as *um* or *uh*. In order to account for the varying length of each review, we normalized the count of all instances of filled pauses by the number of words spoken in the video.
- **Disfluency Markers:** A prominent marker of disfluency in human speech is stuttering. To capture this disfluency, we counted all instances of stuttering in each video and normalized them by the number of words spoken in the video.
- **Articulation Rate:** Articulation rate is defined as the rate of speaking in which all pauses are excluded from calculation (Dankovicova, 1999). This descriptor was computed by taking the ratio of the number of spoken words in each video to the actual time spent speaking.
- **Mean Span of Silence:** Human speech is often interspersed with pauses. We therefore computed this descriptor, by measuring the total duration of silence during speech, normalized by the total length of the video.

5.2 Methodology

We processed all the videos in our dataset and automatically extracted the indicated lexical and paraverbal features. The extracted features were then used for several classification experiments under three different settings to test our hypotheses: only positive reviews, only negative reviews (called the *sentiment-dependent classifiers*) and a combined set of positive and negative reviews (called the *sentiment-independent classifiers*). For each such setting, we divided the set of samples (transcription of movie reviews) into 5 balanced folds that were both speaker-independent and movie-independent. In other words, in all our experiments, no 2 folds contained samples from the same speaker or movie title. This was done to remove any form of bias in the classifier based on either the speaker or the movie.

We then performed classification experiments using 5-fold cross-validation using the lexical features (unigrams and bigrams) on this combined set of reviews (positive and negative reviews together), each time leaving 1 fold for hold-out testing. Here, we note that for constructing the dictionary, only data from the training set was used. On average across 5-fold cross-validation, the number of unigrams was around 4,560 and bigrams around 23,701 for the combined set of movie reviews.

However, since such a feature design typically suffers from problems arising out of the sparsity of the entries of the dictionary in the dataset, we employed a feature selection step. For feature selection and analysis, we used Information Gain (IG), which is a measure of the number of bits of information obtained for category prediction by knowing the presence of a term in a document. Prior evaluation of feature-selection methods for text classification has revealed the superiority of IG as a metric over other ones such as Mutual Information, Term Strength or a simple Document Frequency thresholding for document classification tasks (Yang and Pedersen, 1997). This serves as an inspiring basis for using IG as a metric for feature selection.

The gain score G(t) obtained from IG is a non-zero positive value for features that are strongly indicative of the extent of persuasiveness of the document, while ones that are not so informative have a value of 0. We therefore select only those lexical features (unigrams and bigrams) which have an IG > 0 based on the distribution obtained from the training set. This allows us to trim the dictionary significantly and use only meaningful features for classification.

Feature Group	Sentiment Dependent Classifier			Sentiment Independent Classifier
	Mean	Positive Reviews	Negative Reviews	
Lexical Features (Unigrams and Bigrams)	**83.92%**	81.74%	86.09%	76.73%
• Unigrams Only	**77.70%**	74.78%	80.62%	73.77%
• Bigrams Only	**84.05%**	81.64%	86.46%	75.81%
Para-Linguistic Features	**64.23%**	65.22%	63.23%	63.04%
Early Fusion	**84.54%**	82.61%	86.46%	78.56%
Majority Baseline	52.14%	50.43%	53.85%	51.09%

Table 1: Accuracies for our experiments using a Naïve Bayes classifier. The scores in bold indicate the dominance of the sentiment-dependent classifier under all circumstances.

This was then followed up by a 5-fold cross-validation using only the paraverbal features (no feature selection was used here since they were too few in number). The accuracy of classification based on paraverbal features was then compared with that obtained by classification using only the lexical descriptors and by a majority baseline classifier.

Furthermore, we also tried an early-fusion approach, where we simply use both lexical and paraverbal features together. Such an approach to fusion seemed more promising here than a decision-level fusion approach because of the few categories of features used (just lexical and paralinguistic, as motivated by the findings of (Gunes and Piccardi, 2005)).

5.3 Classification Model

For performing classification experiments we used the Naïve Bayes classifier. A well-known issue with using the Naïve Bayes classifier is its incapability of handling new features, which is handled by performing a conditional uniform smoothing (Puurula, 2012).

6 Results and Discussion

Table 1 shows the results for our classification experiments, which confirm the predictive power of lexical features.

Hypothesis 1: The lexical features (unigrams and bigrams) are predictive of persuasiveness. This is manifested by the fact that they perform significantly better than a majority baseline, which is only 51.04% accurate on the combined set of positive and negative reviews, while the lexical features achieved an accuracy of around 77% (Figure 1). Considering the positive and the negative reviews individually, we note that the lexical features were accurate for nearly 82% of the test samples for the positive reviews and for 86% of the test samples for the negative reviews, again outperforming a simple majority baseline classifier (Table 1).

An analysis of the features (Table 2) reveals that certain lexical features contribute to the predictability of the persuasiveness of a speaker. The presence of unigrams such as *character* or *make* or bigrams such as *to make* or *this movie* for instance, contributes to the predictability of persuasiveness of the speaker, even though they are not emotionally salient terms. The high IG scores of such features irrespective of the setting we conduct our experiments in (positive reviews only, negative reviews only or a combined set of positive and negative reviews), highlights their importance. Moreover, a (+) sign for most of these unigrams or bigrams show that their presence contributes favorably to the speaker being perceived as persuasive. On the other hand a (-) sign for an informative bigram such as *it says* is indicative of lack of speaker's persuasiveness. This can be explained by the context of the usage of such features. For instance, the bigram *it says* in *it says that the movie duration is...* is a bi-

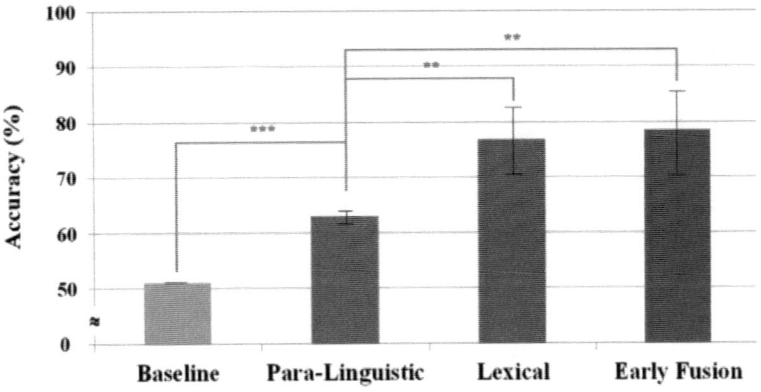

Figure 1: Bar graph visualization of the classification accuracies using different types of features on the combined set of reviews (i.e. sentiment-independent classifier). ** indicates 2-samples t-test results with $p < 0.01$ and *** indicates $p < 0.001$. The error bars show 1 SD.

Feature	Positive Reviews		Negative Reviews		Both Combined	
	Word	IG Score	Word	IG Score	Word	IG Score
Unigrams	The (+)	0.1183	Even (+)	0.11	Make (+)	0.1117
	Make (+)	0.0816	Make (-)	0.1082	Just (+)	0.0728
	Everything (+)	0.0806	Movie (+)	0.0969	Very (+)	0.0669
	Just (+)	0.0806	Real (+)	0.0873	Character (+)	0.0573
	Dollars (+)	0.0722	Not (+)	0.0867	Becomes (+)	0.0558
	Character (+)	0.0685	Big (+)	0.0858	Even (+)	0.0524
	Can (+)	0.0685	One (+)	0.0817	One (+)	0.051
	Product (+)	0.0685	Avoid (+)	0.079	Yourself (+)	0.05
	Famous (+)	0.0609	Feel (+)	0.079	You (+)	0.04571
	Enjoy (+)	0.0566	Character (+)	0.0773	Lot (+)	0.0456
Bigrams	There are (+)	0.1183	This movie (+)	0.1083	To make (+)	0.0905
	This movie (+)	0.0816	Do not (+)	0.1032	A lot (+)	0.0617
	I can't (+)	0.0806	I think (+)	0.1032	This movie (+)	0.0578
	To make (+)	0.0806	To make (+)	0.0989	Lot of (+)	0.0443
	Good movie (+)	0.0722	Not even (+)	0.091	It says (-)	0.0417
	Buy it (+)	0.0685	Don't even (+)	0.091	You will (-)	0.0417
	Really a (+)	0.0685	The story (+)	0.079	Twenty dollars (+)	0.0368
	Definitely one (+)	0.0685	The film (+)	0.0672	The character (+)	0.0386
	Best movies (+)	0.0609	At all (+)	0.0672	So many (+)	0.033
	It's awesome (+)	0.0566	It's so (+)	0.0672	See it (+)	0.033

Table 2: Important unigrams and bigrams when they are used individually as lexical features. (+) indicates that it increases persuasiveness while (-) indicates it contributes to the lack of persuasiveness.

gram that is uttered by the reviewers when they refer to the DVD cover of the movie to give some more detailed information about it. This is identified as a sign of an unpersuasive reviewer. Such results confirm that the verbal behaviors, as captured by lexical usage, are extremely predictive of persuasiveness irrespective of whether the opinion expressed is positive or negative, which validates Hypothesis 1.

Hypothesis 2: Moreover, our experiments show that while the designed paraverbal features that are markers of hesitation can classify only about 63% of the speakers correctly (see Table 1), however

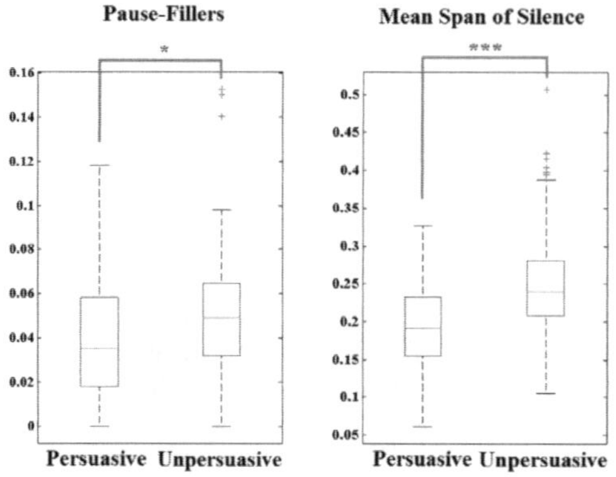

Figure 2: Boxplots for the paralinguistic hesitation markers for a classifier trained on the paralinguistic features only. * and *** indicate p <= 0.05 and 0.001, respectively.

they are statistically significant features, in terms of their p-values (Figure 2). While classification performance is lower than that obtained with purely lexical features, it is still far above a majority baseline, and thus confirms our second hypothesis.

Additionally, it is interesting to note from Table 1 that, although a feature-level fusion of the lexical features and paraverbal features gives us an improvement in classification performance, the difference between the results obtained with fusion and those with lexical features alone was minor and was not statistically significant.

Hypothesis 3: We also observe that a sentiment-dependent classifier trained individually on positive reviews or on negative reviews outperforms one that is trained on a combined set of reviews. This is supported by our empirical results in Table 1 which show that when classification is performed with any of the lexical features, the accuracies are significantly higher for the classifier trained only on the positive or only on the negative reviews (sentiment-dependent classifiers) than for the classifier trained on the combined set of reviews (sentiment-independent classifiers). For instance, when unigrams and bigrams were both used as our lexical features, we observed that for a sentiment-dependent classifier the classification accuracy jumps to over 84% on average. This is significantly better than the scenario where the classifier is not aware of the sentiment of the review. Figure 3 demonstrates this phenomenon.

We resort to feature analysis for an explanation of such an observation (Table 2). The analysis reveals that certain sentiment-based lexical features, i.e. emotionally salient terms, assume an important role in magnifying the discriminative power of language use in persuasiveness prediction, when prior knowledge about the speaker's opinion is known. For instance, in the case of a classifier trained only on the positive reviews, unigrams such as *enjoy* and *famous* and bigrams such as *good movie* or *it's awesome* become significant. In the context of persuading against watching the movie prominent sentiment-based unigrams are *not* and *avoid* while bigrams are *do not*, *don't even* and *at all*. This provides empirical support for our third hypothesis.

7 Conclusion and Future Work

This work presents several interesting findings about perceived persuasiveness prediction in online social multimedia content by analyzing the verbal behavior of the speaker, modeled using lexical features and paraverbal features of hesitation. We conducted experiments and showed that verbal behavior as captured by lexical descriptors is a strong indicator of persuasiveness, irrespective of whether we persuade in favor of or against something. Much of this is due to the presence of certain unigrams and bigrams that are either indicative of strong persuasiveness or of lack of persuasiveness. Our experiments further reveal the superiority of classifying with lexical features as compared to with para-

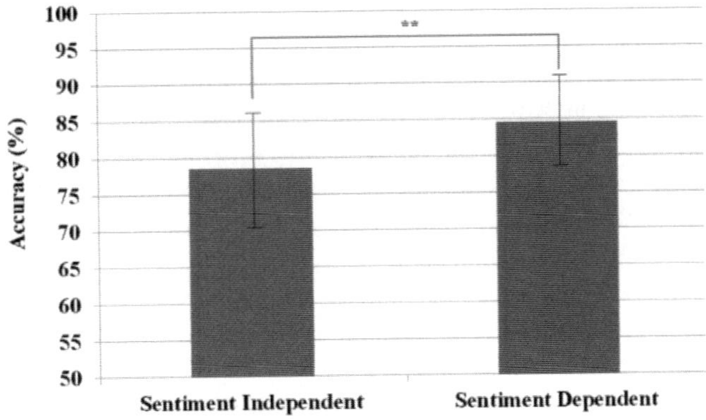

Figure 3: Bar graph visualization of the classification accuracies of lexical features using a sentiment-dependent classifier (mean) and a sentiment independent one. ** indicates 2-sample t-test results with $p < 0.01$ and the error bars show 1 SD.

verbal features alone. Moreover we empirically validate the hypothesis that a sentiment-aware classifier outperforms a sentiment-independent one. As future work, we intend to explore more paraverbal features for persuasiveness prediction and also try more sophisticated prediction models which explicitly model the temporal dynamic.

Acknowledgments

This work was supported by the National Science Foundation under Grant IIS-1118018 and the U.S. Army. The content does not necessarily reflect the position or the policy of the Government, and no official endorsement should be inferred.

References

Shelly Chaiken and Alice H. Eagly. 1979. Communication modality as a determinant of message persuasiveness and message comprehensibility. *Journal of Personality and Social Psychology*, 37:1387-1397.

Jana Dankovicova. 1999. Articulation rate variation within the intonation phrase in Czech and English. *14th Int. Congress of Phonetic Sciences*, San Francisco, Vol. 1, pp. 269-272.

Kushal Dave, Steve Lawrence, and David M. Pennck. Mining the Peanut Gallery: Opinion Extraction and semantic Classification of Product Reviews, 2003. *2003 Association for Computational Linguistics (ACL '03).*

David DeVault, Kallirroi Georgila, Ron Artstein, Fabrizio Morbini, David Traum, Stefan, Scherer, Albert (Skip) Rizzo, and Louis-Philippe Morency. 2013. Verbal indicators of psychological distress in interactive dialogue with a virtual human. *SIGDIAL 2013 Conf, 2013 Association for Computational Linguistics (ACL '13).*

Laurence Devillers and Laurence Vidrascu. 2006. Real-life emotions detection with lexical and paralinguistric cues on Human-Human call center dialogs. *Interspeech 2006.*

Hatice Gunes, and Massimo Piccardi. 2005. Affect Recognition from face and body: Early fusion vs. Late fusion. *IEEE Int'l Conf. on Systems, Man and Cybernnetic.*

Daniel J. O'Keefe. 2002. *Persuasion: Theory and research.* (2nd Edition). Sage Publications, Thousand Oaks, CA.

David D. Lewis and William A. Gale. 1994. A Sequential Algorithm for Training Text Classifiers. *Special Interest Group in Information Retieval (SIGIR'94).*

Gerald R. Miller (1980). *On being persuaded: Some basic distinctions.* In M. Roloff, & G. R. Miller (Eds.), Persuasion: New directions in theory and research, 11–28. Beverly Hills, CA: Sage.

Tom M. Mitchell. 1997. *Machine Learning*. McGraw-Hill.

Gelareh Mohammadi, Sunghyun Park, Kenji Sagae, Alessandro Vinciarelli, and Lois-Phillippe Morency. 2013. Who is persuasive? The role of perceived personality and Communication modality in social multimedia. *Int'l Conf. on Multimodal Interfaces (ICMI '13).*

P. Karen Murphy. 2001. What makes a text persuasive? Comparing students' and experts' conceptions of persuasiveness. *Int'l Journal of Education Research*, 35 (2001) 675-698.

Bo Pang, Lillian Lee, and Shivakumar Vaithyanathan. 2002. Thumbs up? Sentiment Classification using Machine Learning Techniques. *Conf. on Empirical Methods in Natural Language Processing. (EMNLP '02).*

Antti Puurula. 2012. *Combining Modifications to Multinomial Naive Bayes for Text Classification.* Springer, LNCS.

Kathleen Kelley Reardon. 1991. *Persuasion in practice.* Sage Publication, Inc.

Carol Werner. 1982. Intrusiveness and persuasive impact of three communication media. *Journal of Applied Social Psychology,* 89:155-181.

Yiming Yang and Jan O. Pedersen. 1997. A comparative study on feature selection in text categorization. *Int'l Conf. on Machine Learning (ICML '97).*

Joel Young, Craig Martell, Pranav Anand, Pedro Ortiz and Henry T. Gilbert IV. 2011. A Microtext Corpus for Persuasion Detection in Dialog. *Analyzing Microtext: AAAI Workshop (AAAI-Workshop '11).*

Phillip G. Zimbardo and Michael R. Leippe. 1991. *The psychology of attitude change and social influence.* McGrew-Hill New York.

Content+Context=Classification: Examining the Roles of Social Interactions and Linguist Content in Twitter User Classification*

W. M. Campbell
Human Language Technology
MIT Lincoln Laboratory
Lexington, MA 01740
wcampbell@ll.mit.edu

E. Baseman†
School of Computer Science
Univ. of Mass. Amherst
Amherst, MA 01003
ebaseman@cs.umass.edu

K. Greenfield
Human Language Technology
MIT Lincoln Laboratory
Lexington, MA 01740
kara.greenfield@ll.mit.edu

Abstract

Twitter users demonstrate many characteristics via their online presence. Connections, community memberships, and communication patterns reveal both idiosyncratic and general properties of users. In addition, the content of tweets can be critical for distinguishing the role and importance of a user. In this work, we explore Twitter user classification using context and content cues. We construct a rich graph structure induced by hashtags and social communications in Twitter. We derive features from this graph structure—centrality, communities, and local flow of information. In addition, we perform detailed content analysis on tweets looking at offensiveness and topics. We then examine user classification and the role of feature types (context, content) and learning methods (propositional, relational) through a series of experiments on annotated data. Our work contrasts with prior approaches in that we use relational learning and alternative, non-specialized feature sets. Our goal is to understand how both content and context are predictive of user characteristics. Experiments demonstrate that the best performance for user classification uses relational learning with varying content and context features.

1 Introduction

In recent years, Twitter has become an extremely prolific social media engine, attracting an extremely diverse user base, ranging from teenagers discussing the latest in pop culture, to businesses looking for free advertising space, to the president of the United States trying to reach a broader audience than traditional media will allow. Twitter is the place to say whatever you want to whoever you want..., as long as it is less than 140 characters. This conciseness constraint forced the Twitter user base to develop innovative ways of maximizing the information content of each letter. As such, the resulting tweets constitute a vast data set of rich textual content. Additionally, these tweets traverse through and define a social network comprised of all kinds of people tweeting to people about people.

In this work, we try to identify who some of these people are by performing user classification. Several prior methods have been proposed. Teng and Chen (2006) performed a similar study on bloggers in order to classify them by interest type. Twitter, however, provides a much richer feature set due to the denser network structure and nearly ubiquitous adoption of user profiles. Romero et al. (2011) defined a social graph structure for Twitter data. While this was the first paper of its kind to explore the benefits of extracting a network structure from textual data, they only considered a limited graph comprising the retweet structure. Rao et al. (2010) and Pennacchiotti and Popescu (2011) expanded the notion of a Twitter graph to more broadly encompass social communication and used this jointly with content features to predict some attributes of Twitter users. Only limited graph analysis was performed and

†This work was performed under an internship at MIT Lincoln Laboratory.

*This work was sponsored by the Defense Advanced Research Projects Agency under Air Force Contract FA8721-05-C-0002. Opinions, interpretations, conclusions, and recommendations are those of the authors and are not necessarily endorsed by the United States Government.

Proceedings of the Second Workshop on Natural Language Processing for Social Media (SocialNLP), pages 59–65, Dublin, Ireland, August 24 2014.

learning was based on the user and not relational methods. In (Wu et al., 2011), a special feature, Twitter lists, was used as a simple approach to user classification.

Our goal is to explore the role of different features and learning methods in user classification. The motivation for this study is multifold. First, prior work has only performed limited analysis on Twitter graph structures and their role in user characterization. Second, the interplay between content, context, and learning method (relational versus propositional) has not been fully explored. Third, user classification using profile information or specific Twitter features may not always be available or accurate. In our study, we find 20% of the users do not have an accessible profile. Additionally, since profile information contains self-reported fields, its accuracy is questionable.

In this paper, our contribution consists of multiple parts. First, we develop a rich network representation of Twitter data that combines the traditionally exploited social network features (retweeting, at-mentions), user tweeting behaviors (hashtag usage), and hashtag co-occurrence without requiring storage of all tweets. We perform network analysis on this graph and show that community structure and centrality in the network are qualitatively interesting and relevant for user classification. Second, we perform tweet level topic clustering and offensiveness detection. We propose a new method for propagating posterior class probabilities to both hashtag and at-mention graph nodes. This provides topic and offensiveness associations for both users and hashtags in the Twitter graph. Finally, in constrast to prior work, we perform relational learning on the Twitter graph and show significant improvements in performance by using information from hashtag-neighbors and user-neighbors of a user node.

2 Corpus Collection

Over the 8 month period from September 2012 to March 2013, we used Twitter's streaming API to collect a $< 1\%$ sample of the entire twitter feed, totaling approximately 686 million tweets, which (Morstatter et al., 2013) showed to be a representative sample of the entire Twitter space. These tweets contain basic information—tweet id, date and time, user id, user location, and tweet text. The tweets are representative of the Twitter population and display a wide variety of user accounts, topics, languages, and locations.

In addition to collecting a corpus of tweets, we used Twitter's REST API to collect the user profiles for all users who were either an author of or at-mentioned in at least one of the previously collected tweets. User profiles contain both user generated and automatically generated content. The user generated content includes information such as webpage link, location, time zone, screen name, language, and a textual description of the account. Since these are self-reported attributes, their veracity is often noisy or over-generalized—e.g., location reported as "all around the world." The automatically generated user account content consists of account information and statistics such as number of followers, date of account creation, number of tweets (statuses_count), verified status, and favorite count.

We augmented our tweet + profile corpus by labeling a subset of user profiles with their user type. Annotation was performed by multiple annotators. We considered the following partitioning of user profiles into user classes. **individual:famous** : Famous person: writer, actor, former politician, etc. **individual:generic** : Generic (everyday) user tweeting. **individual:other** : An individual that doesn't fall into the categories above. **organization** : Business, non-profit, government organization. **fake** : Fictional characters, celebrity impersonations, deceased individuals, etc. **info** : Information source–news, trivia, jokes, quotes. **bots** : Produces automated posts via Twitter. **missing** : User doesn't exist (deleted page or misspelled user id). **dontcare** : Spam, offensive services. **other** : Not in one of the above categories. We selected this schema as an initial exploration of interesting categories and many alternate schema are possible.

3 Twitter Graph Construction

In order to construct an analytics platform, we applied a mapping that converts a corpus of tweets and corresponding user profiles into a Twitter graph. There are several methods of representing Twitter data as a graph which capture diferent levels of data richness at inversely proportional computational expense (both in processing and storage requirements). In this work, we consider a graph with multityped nodes in one-to-one correspondence with the union of the set of user profiles (e.g., `@blueman`) and the set of

Table 1: Example communities obtained from Infomap community detection with the Twitter Graph

Communities and High-Pagerank Members	Highest Pagerank Node
#me, #cute, #instagood, #beautiful, #fashion	#love
#500aday, #tfb, #instantfollowback, #teamautofollow, #followback	#teamfollowback
#breakoutartist, #musicfans, #onedirection, #popartist, #celebrityjudge	#peopleschoice
#android, #androidgames, #ipad, #ipadgames, #iphone	#gamesinsight
@harry_styles, @real_liam_payne, @louis_tomlinson, @zaynmalik, @onedirection	@niallofficial
#football, #49ers, #packers, #ravens, #redskins	#nfl
#p2, #teaparty, #tlot, #gop, #obama	#tcot
#believecoustic, #believe, #believetour, #kiss, @alfredoflores	@justinbieber

hashtags (e.g., #yankees) that occur in one or more of the collected tweets. We chose not to include individual tweets as nodes in the graph in order to maintain tractability.

In addition to the two classes of nodes, we considered five classes of edges. There are three classes of edges that connect two user profile nodes. The first is a directed, weighted edge corresponding to the number of times one user at-mentions another user (e.g., @blueman writes a tweet containing @greenman). The second type of user to user edge is a directed, weighted edge corresponding to the number of times one user retweets another user (e.g., @blueman writes a tweet containing RT @greenman). Unlike the at-mentions and retweets edges, the third type of user to user edge doesn't map to communication between users; rather this edge classification refers to an undirected, weighted count of the number of times at-mentions of two users co-occur in the same tweet (e.g., @redman writes a tweet containing @greenman and @blueman). Similarly to the user to user co-occurence edge classification, there is an undirected, weighted edge classification corresponding to the co-occurrence of two hashtags. The final class of edges are weighted, directed edges corresponding to the number of times a given user tweets a particular hashtag.

4 Graph Features

We extracted network features from the Twitter graph based on community detection and centrality (Pagerank). We partitioned the node set into commuties by leveraging the infomap approach (Rosvall and Bergstrom, 2008). We use Pagerank to calculate the centrality of each node and we define community centrality as the sum of the Pageranks for all nodes in the community. The community "Pagerank" allows us to rank communities by centrality. After computing both Pagerank and communities, we added these node features to the original (directed) graph.

Optimizing the communities in the Twitter graph yields communities with both user and hashtag nodes. Nodes with high-pagerank in a community serve as a community summarizations. We show a summary of some of the largest Pagerank sum communities in Table 1. Cursory analysis reveals that qualitatively the communities are very interpretable—user Justin Bieber is associated with the Believe tour, the hashtag #gameinsight is associated with different platforms and game types, followbacks are grouped together, and the #love community has the highest community Pagerank.

5 Content Analysis

Content analysis uses natural language processing to extract additional structured features from unstructured tweets. We discussed simple content analysis based on parsing tweets in order to identify communication (at-mentions and retweets) and content (hashtags) in a previous section. In this section, we cover more advanced techniques—topic modeling and offensiveness detection.

Before covering the details of content analysis, we describe the general framework for incorporating content features into our classification framework. We assume that content analysis produces a vector of posterior probabilities,

$$\mathbf{c}_j = \left[p(\omega_i|\text{tweet}_j)\right] \tag{1}$$

where ω_i is the indicator for the class label i. In general, including all tweets as nodes in a graph for classification leads to a graph of prohibitive size. Instead, we propagate the information contained in tweets to corresponding user and hashtag nodes and compute the expected posterior probability; i.e., we average all of the vectors propagated to a certain node.

The rules for propagating $\mathbf{c}_j$ for at-mentions are as follows. If user `@blueman` tweets with no recipient or multiple recipients, then $\mathbf{c}_j$ is propagated to the `@blueman` node. If user `@blueman` retweets from user `@greenman`, then $\mathbf{c}_j$ is propagated to both `@blueman` and `@greenman`. Similarly for hashtags nodes, we propagate the $\mathbf{c}_j$ vector to all hashtags used in tweet_j.

Averaging the content vectors that were propagated to user and hashtag nodes defines representative content vectors for those nodes. A drawback of this aggregation strategy is that the average estimator can have a variable variance proportional to the number of vectors propagated to a node, which can introduce noise into the classification process.

5.1 Topic Modeling

Our topic modeling is based upon probabilistic latent semantic analysis (PLSA). PLSA models the joint probability between documents and words by introducing a latent variable z representing possible topics in a document. We trained the PLSA model with an EM algorithm.

An analysis of the topics produced by PLSA provides meaningful interpretation of many of the high scoring topics. For instance, topics such as money, sleep habits, the ubiquitous Justin Bieber, birthdays and Valentine's day, and love are easily seen. Expressions of happiness via emoticons are also a topic. The topics in general represent broad categories (love, football) and specific events (video awards, Valentine's day). In addition, topics that represent common linguistic phenomena—African American vernacular English (AAVE), various expletives, and teen lifestyle (class, teacher, parents, ...). We remark that the topics are related to but not the same as the community detection applied to the Twitter graph. Qualitatively, the Twitter graph communities appear to be better defined and more easily interpreted than their PLSA counterparts.

5.2 Offensiveness

Another significant attribute of a tweet is linguistic register—the variation due to the social setting. In an attempt to capture some of the phenomena that occurs due to formality, familiarity, etc., we trained an offensiveness detector. The goal of building this detector is that variations in offensiveness might distinguish user type (e.g., politician versus generic user).

Offensiveness is a broad term and could be defined in many different ways. We define offensiveness using a pragmatic two-stage approach. First, we obtained a set of offensive tweets by issuing queries via Lucene of offensive terms. To obtain a set of putative non-offensive tweets, we took a random sample of the remaining tweets from a large pool, assuming that in this case offensiveness has a lower prior. We then trained a classifier with the offensive and non-offensive data sets. The resulting output of the detector yields a consistent definition of offensiveness. Additionally, training a detector rather than using just a dictionary approach captures some of the additional co-occurring terms and allows learning appropriate weightings of terms.

We split the annotated data into distinct train and test sets for performance measurement and calibration of the detector. Approximately 14000 tweets were in both sets. We trained an SVM by using normalized word-count vectors and a linear kernel. The SVM regularization parameter was tuned for optimal performance to $c = 0.1$. The equal error rate is 12.4% for the detector. The detector appears to produce consistent results. Given that tweets are short messages, this performance level appears reasonable.

We needed two additional steps in order to apply the detector to all English tweets. First, we converted the output of the SVM to a posterior probability using the standard approach in Platt (Platt, 2000) and optimized by using a conjugate gradient method. Second, there were numerous cases in the data where unseen vocabulary in the training set resulted in a zero-vector for $\mathbf{v}_i$. In these cases, we used an imputed posterior of offensiveness by taking the average value across all nodes.

6 User Classification

Our goal in this work is to identify the saliency of network and content features as well as relational versus propositional learning methods for classifying Twitter users. We cast the user classication problem as a detection problem; i.e., for each label (verified, generic, etc.), we build a 1-versus-rest detector to predict that attribute of the user.

Since our representation of the Twitter data involves user-user, user-hashtag, and hashtag-hashtag relationships, we apply a relational learning approach to user classification. Relational learning techniques leverage the structure of the neighborhood around a user of interest as well as the attributes of that user and its neighbors. In this work, we construct queries consisting of the user of interest, and the nodes adjacent to and edges incident to that user. We use relational probability trees (RPTs) (Neville et al., 2003) to leverage these subgraphs for classification. An RPT is a decision tree which automatically calculates and considers aggregate features within the subgraphs.

7 Experiments

7.1 Experimental Setup

From a 1% sample of raw tweets, we created a Twitter graph combining content and network features. We included network structure in the graph by letting edges indicate retweets, communication and co-occurance of users in tweets, or co-occurrence of hashtags within tweets. In addition, we annotated each edge with counts for each interaction type. We added additional content features for topic and offensiveness as well as network features for cluster and cluster pagerank for each user and hashtag. Topic vectors were assigned using a PLSA approach, and offensiveness was determined using an SVM. Clustering and pagerank were achieved using the infomap approach. In addition, we hand-annotated approximately 1300 users (individual:famous, individual:generic, individual:other, organization, info source, bot, etc.) by examining their profiles and tweets. The resulting graph had 252K nodes (189K users and 64K hashtags), and 1.16M edges.

We performed experiments using multiple feature subsets (content, network and content+network) and different learning methods (propositional, relational). The content features we generated for users and hashtags are topic and offensiveness. We include the top three most likely topics for each user and hashtag in our feature set for these experiments. Our network features for users and hashtags are cluster and cluster pagerank. We cast the user classification process as a detection problem. For each user label (verified, generic, etc.), we create a detector using an RPT that uses a one-versus-rest labeling.

To predict whether or not a user has a verified account, we learn decision trees with Proximity* with varying features included in the analysis. There were a total of 84k users with a verified label in our graph from downloaded Twitter profiles. We subsampled 10% of this data set to give reasonable run times for Proximity.

For the remaining hand-annotated classes, we used all available labeled data. We learned decision trees using Proximity with a maximum tree depth of 3. For some user types, there were not enough labeled users to make reliable models and predictions; we excluded user types with probability less than or equal to 1% (fake, other, spam). We also found prediction of organization to be unreliable. Therefore, we focused our experiments on high-prior hand-annotated classes—generic, info, and famous.

For both relational and propositional (user-only) learning, we divided the data into 5 random splits with 80% of the data in training and 20% of the data in test. For each split, we measured the area under the curve (AUC) from the trained detector on the heldout test set. Results are reported in terms of the mean and standard deviation (SD) of the AUC across all splits.

Relational learning was somewhat complicated by the varying structure of user neighborhoods. Ideally, we would like our graph queries to return subgraphs that consist of a central labeled user, and all users and hashtags that are immediate neighbors of this labeled user. However, the RPTs need to be able to calculate the same aggregate features for each subgraph. A problem arises because some labeled user nodes only have neighbors that are users, while other user nodes have only hashtag neighbors, and still

*Software and documentation is available at http://kdl.cs.umass.edu/proximity

more nodes have both user and hashtag neighbors. There is also an unusual case where some users do not have any neighbors. We find that user nodes from these four neighborhood structure cases (no neighbors, only user neighbors, only hashtag neighbors, and both user and hashtag neighbors) cannot all be mixed together in the same training and test sets. This diffculty occurs because aggregate attributes that are well-defined on the users with only hashtag neighbors, such as average offensiveness of neighboring hashtags, are undefined for nodes with only user neighbors. We handle this by running separate sets of experiments for each of these four neighborhood structure cases.

7.2 User Classification Experiments

7.2.1 Verified User Results

Table 2 shows average AUC results for propositional and relational prediction of account verification. Note that an AUC of 0.5 indicates chance performance. From the table, we see that we can perform reasonable user classification of verified users using our *extracted* features.

From the table, we can reach multiple conclusions. First, propositional learning performs similarly with either network-only or content-only features. Second, content and network features together provide a significant boost in performance. This observation has been noted in other domains such as Enron e-mail (Coppersmith and Priebe, 2012). Third, the introduction of relational learning gives substantial performance improvements over propositional learning. For instance, the performance of content features is substantially increased in the relational case with "users only." A fourth observation is that "not all neighbors are created equal." In all cases, the use of information about user neighbors is substantially more important than hashtag neighbors. We found that most neighborhoods contained users; the distribution was none (11%), user only (43%), hashtag only (9%), and both (37%).

7.2.2 Hand-Annotated Results

Additional experiments on the three labels famous, generic, and info were also performed and results are shown in Table 2. Note that the small number of labels is most likely impacting two aspects of performance. First, since we have a smaller training set size, best absolute AUC is typically lower than the verified case. Also, in some cases performance is worse than chance showing that it is difficult to generalize well from a small training set. In general, though, similar trends in AUC performance are similar to the verified case.

For both the famous and generic labels with propositional learning, we found that network-only features work substantially better than content-only features. For info labels, content-only features are slightly better demonstrating that info is a unique case.

Further examination of relational results shows similar trends to the verified user case. Relational methods are superior to propositional methods. In addition, using both network and content features is helpful or at least not detrimental to performance. The case of the info user class is interesting from the viewpoint of neighbors; we see that the gap in performance between hashtag-only neighbors and user-only neighbors is less than other user classes. In terms of features appearing in the RPTs, we found that all features were valuable in user classification. Aggregate features were common as decision points in the relational case.

8 Conclusions

Twitter contains a rich set of social network, content, and individual user cues that give insight into user characteristics. In this paper, we explored features that captured these characteristics via topic clustering, offensiveness detection, and network analytics. Additionally, we examined various classification strategies which used both propositional and relational methods. Our different approaches demonstrated that the different feature types are complementary and all indicative of user classification. For example, finding "interesting" Twitter accounts (the opposite of generic users) can be accomplished with content and network features. This process emphasizes the fact that user classification can be accomplished with many strategies. Possible future work includes performing alternative classification studies, analyzing the effects of different sample sizes, extending to other languages, and predicting additional user classes.

Table 2: Average and standard deviation AUC for detection of verified and annotated accounts. Propositional results are indicated by a "-" in neighborhood structure.

Feature Sets	Neighborhood Structure	Verified AUC Avg (SD)	Famous AUC Avg (SD)	Generic AUC Avg (SD)	Info AUC Avg (SD)
Content	-	0.6201 (0.0219)	0.5549 (0.0215)	0.5725 (0.0390)	0.7716 (0.0436)
Network	-	0.6916 (0.0339)	0.7685 (0.0529)	0.7110 (0.0468)	0.6438 (0.0791)
Content+Network	-	0.7443 (0.0349)	0.7901 (0.0136)	0.7301 (0.0290)	0.7002 (0.1682)
Content	No Neighbors	0.5935 (0.0306)	0.5970 (0.1583)	0.5842 (0.1535)	0.4006 (0.1777)
Content	Users Only	0.8945 (0.0248)	0.8172 (0.0375)	0.7558 (0.0560)	0.6813 (0.1321)
Content	Hashtags Only	0.6501 (0.0416)	0.4939 (0.1548)	0.5557 (0.1518)	0.6153 (0.1151)
Content	Users and Hashtags	0.9213 (0.0202)	0.8420 (0.0564)	0.7790 (0.0589)	0.5583 (0.0954)
Network	No Neighbors	0.5123 (0.1292)	0.6227 (0.1707)	0.4085 (0.0505)	0.4040 (0.1224)
Network	Users Only	0.8760 (0.0310)	0.8383 (0.0262)	0.7708 (0.0527)	0.6433 (0.1336)
Network	Hashtags Only	0.4821 (0.0657)	0.4502 (0.1418)	0.5995 (0.0576)	0.5778 (0.1241)
Network	Users and Hashtags	0.9091 (0.0257)	0.8437 (0.0157)	**0.8014** (0.0559)	**0.8038** (0.0760)
Content+Network	No Neighbors	0.5939 (0.0801)	0.5654 (0.1141)	0.6572 (0.1299)	0.3917 (0.1487)
Content+Network	Users Only	0.8823 (0.0317)	0.8019 (0.0520)	0.7566 (0.0474)	0.5815 (0.1708)
Content+Network	Hashtags Only	0.6699 (0.0525)	0.4510 (0.1312)	0.5543 (0.0954)	0.4260 (0.2057)
Content+Network	Users and Hashtags	**0.9325** (0.0087)	**0.8431** (0.0535)	0.7831 (0.0192)	0.8021 (0.0608)

References

Glen A Coppersmith and Carey E Priebe. 2012. Vertex nomination via content and context. *arXiv preprint arXiv:1201.4118*.

Fred Morstatter, Jurgen Pfeffer, Huan Liu, and Kathleen M Carley. 2013. Is the sample good enough? comparing data from twitter's streaming api with twitter's firehose. *Proceedings of ICWSM*.

Jennifer Neville, David D. Jensen, Lisa Friedland, and Michael Hay. 2003. Learning relational probability trees. In Lise Getoor, Ted E. Senator, Pedro Domingos, and Christos Faloutsos, editors, *Proceedings of the Ninth ACM SIGKDD International Conference on Knowledge Discovery and Data Mining*, pages 625–630, Washington, DC, August. ACM Press, New York, NY. Poster session: Research track.

Marco Pennacchiotti and Ana-Maria Popescu. 2011. A machine learning approach to twitter user classification. In *ICWSM*.

John C. Platt. 2000. Probabilities for SV machines. In Alexander J. Smola, Peter L. Bartlett, Bernhard Schölkopf, and Dale Schuurmans, editors, *Advances in Large Margin Classifiers*, pages 61–74. The MIT Press.

Delip Rao, David Yarowsky, Abhishek Shreevats, and Manaswi Gupta. 2010. Classifying latent user attributes in twitter. In *Proceedings of the 2nd international workshop on Search and mining user-generated contents*, pages 37–44. ACM.

Daniel M Romero, Wojciech Galuba, Sitaram Asur, and Bernardo A Huberman. 2011. Influence and passivity in social media. In *Machine learning and knowledge discovery in databases*, pages 18–33. Springer.

Martin Rosvall and Carl T. Bergstrom. 2008. Maps of random walks on complex networks reveal community structure. *Proceedings of the National Academy of Sciences*.

Chun-Yuan Teng and Hsin-Hsi Chen. 2006. Detection of bloggers' interests: using textual, temporal, and interactive features. In *Proceedings of the 2006 IEEE/WIC/ACM International Conference on Web Intelligence*, pages 366–369. IEEE Computer Society.

Shaomei Wu, Jake M Hofman, Winter A Mason, and Duncan J Watts. 2011. Who says what to whom on twitter. In *Proceedings of the 20th international conference on World wide web*, pages 705–714. ACM.

Author Index